AT THE POINT OF A KNIFE

A memoir about a life-saving invention, the hijacking of a hi-tech start- up, and the explosive meltdown of a nuclear family

By: **Kenneth Richard Fox**

Pachyderm Press

pachydermenterprises7@gmail.com

Kenneth Fox

ACKNOWLEDGMENT

Thanks to Barbara Sopkin for the many hours she devoted to improving this manuscript.

CHAPTER 1

It was still a little before eight on a chilly Monday morning in the autumn of 1992, but the Albert V. Bryan, Sr. U.S. Federal Courthouse in Alexandria, Virginia was already abuzz with activity. International terrorists, infamous spies and other notorious characters had been tried in this courthouse over the years, and there had been monumental corporate struggles here as well. Today, it was our turn. Earlier that morning, Art and I had been helping our four lawyers move boxes of documents into a small second-floor courtroom that would become the center of our existence for the next week. Our opponents, with their forty-two attorneys from Washington, D.C., Los Angeles and Chicago, had already assembled dozens of boxes of documents they intended to use to destroy us.

Fourteen years earlier, around Christmas time, Dr. Art Coster had approached me at the hospital one day. Art was a Holocaust survivor and a fellow department chairman at the hospital. He had watched me do eye surgery with a laser on a few occasions. He had done research on diseased blood vessels and wondered whether laser energy could clear the arterial blockages that cause heart attack and stroke. He was not the first to ask that question, nor were we the first to investigate that possibility. But, nearly four years later, we were the first to discover how to accomplish this feat without damaging the blood vessel walls.

During those years, Art and I and our little array of consultants in laser physics, pathology, cardiology and other disciplines, fired lasers inside cadaver blood vessels and at animal tissue models time and time again until we stumbled upon the right combination of energy parameters.

I spoke to a patent attorney whose little boy was in my daughter's play group. Our discussion led to seven tumultuous years in and out of government patent offices in Washington, Tokyo, Munich, Paris, Toronto, Canberra and Seoul. A small army of international patent lawyers fought for the various national patent examiners to recognize our invention in the blood vessel, or intraluminal areas, as novel and broadly patentable, so as to allow our claims.

Advanced Interventional Systems, known by its stock ticker LAIS, was a textbook example of a start-up medical device company. It had been selling a medical device based on our technology for a couple of years. The medical instrument was used to thread through small blood vessels tiny catheters filled with fiber-optic transmitters of controllable laser energy to remove dangerous blockages. Those obstructions were caused by arteriosclerotic plaques, which build up over time. The instrument was a life saver, and it utilized the laser energy that we had invented and patented. This process was called "laser angioplasty," a name we had in our patent applications. The manufacturers changed the name to "laser atherectomy" when they fought to avoid paying us royalties.

A medical tech start-up is typically founded by someone with a scientific idea for use in medicine or someone with a good friend who happened to have one. If the product is a medical device, the founders usually build prototypes and get advice from friends or associates practicing in the relevant medical fields. The fledgling companies wrap themselves up in a business plan with attractive bells and whistles.

In the heady days of the 1980s and '90s , after two or three rounds of successive venture capital groups buying into the concept, a company could make a fast annual return of as much as 100% or more on the ten or fifteen million dollars of its original seed money. The start-up could find aggressive investment bankers who would organize an initial public offering (IPO) and the shares would usually trade on the NASDAQ exchange. Everyone who had gotten in near the beginning came out a quick winner.

Because investor funding was abundantly available, there were many such successes. Genentech, in the biotech field, was an example of an enormous and rapid success story from that time.

Advanced Interventional Systems might not have been a household name, but it had gotten a fast start via the public equity market and was on its way. The number of people whose lives it might improve or even save was enormous.

These medical start-ups were the mirror image, albeit usually on a smaller scale, of the hi- tech, non- medical revolution of the times, with fast money and success or stunning failure.

But that Monday morning Art and I were not in that storied Virginia courthouse to celebrate our successes. We were fighting for our invention and our survival in innovative medical technology. We had invented and patented technology for preventing and treating heart attacks and strokes in a safer, effective manner. LAIS had copied it, engineered it into their laser and catheter systems for blood vessel interventional surgery and was selling it without our authorization. They were stealing it.

LAIS management had ignored our requests that they license our technology for a fair royalty, enabling them to use our invention legally. They thought that it would be cheaper and easier to destroy us. We were determined to prove how shortsighted they had been.

By ten o'clock, the trial was ready to begin before federal district court Judge Albert V. Bryan, Jr. The courthouse had been named after this senior judge's father, a respected justice from the Virginia federal bench. Judge Bryan the younger, already around retirement age, had a reputation for not cutting lawyers any slack. He was also known for his intellect, honesty and fairness. At that time, I did not know how rare that combination was. Not going to be manipulated by the attorneys before him, Judge Bryan was going to impart justice his way, and quickly.

In the Eastern District of Virginia, the so- called "rocket docket," even a complicated patent infringement case such as ours was given only four trial days. In other U.S. federal courts, this trial might have taken years to start and then dragged on for months; ours began only months after it had been filed. We had chosen this federal court district partly for its alacrity. Endless delays probably would have suited LAIS, which had a vast litigation budget; we could never have survived the financial ordeal.

Art and I had already worked for more than ten years in our spare time on experiments and on the agonizing back-and-forth patenting process in the United States and beyond. The patent effort was spearheaded by the astute and diligent George Myers.

Art and I also paid the world expert in the physical scattering properties of light, Dr. Robert Gammon of the University of Maryland, and others to help with the laser physics in our technology.

I had spent countless hours gathering industry intelligence about cardiac and other clinical problems, competing technologies, world markets for these types of medical devices, reimbursement methods of governmental and private medical insurers in major Western countries, U.S. Food and Drug Administration (FDA), European Union (EU) and other regulatory bodies' requirements for medical-device approvals and other relevant information. We had to learn everything there was to know about our industry.

Art and I had been self- financing our project for about a dozen years before this trial. We had spent approximately two years in planning and initial research. We worked for another seven years or so on international patenting and appeals and another three years in initial patent licensing and the first of many patent- related lawsuits.

In that Alexandria, Virginia, courtroom it was about five minutes to midnight for us.

CHAPTER 2

About eight years after the beginning of our work, Art and I formed a company called PILLCO ("Pulsed Intraluminal Laser Company") that held the patents and licensed our technology exclusively to a large player in the medical device industry. The licensee was USCI, the cardiology technology division of C.R. Bard in New Jersey. USCI had a large share of the lucrative balloon angioplasty market, the non- laser predecessor to laser angioplasty. That world-wide market was worth billions of dollars a year in sales, mostly of disposable, single- use catheters for treating patients with arteriosclerotic vascular disease.

By the late 1980s, Art and I saw the potential to expand the usage of our technology to capture a significant share of the market for clearing blockages in popliteal and femoral arteries of the legs, cerebral arteries supplying the brain and other significant vessels responsible for blood circulation.

The appeal of the growing market for clearing blood vessel blockages was already so great that just a few years later C. R. Bard, motivated by greed, would plead guilty to the then largest medical criminal fraud case ever brought by the U.S. government against any manufacturer. The charges concerned the company's sales of a device to remove coronary artery blockages. C.R. Bard paid a huge criminal fine and lost its share of the balloon angioplasty market.

Before the fraud was uncovered, Art and I were convinced that USCI wanted to engineer, develop and commercialize our technology to improve their product line with the cutting edge in interventional cardiology, interventional vascular surgery and interventional radiology.

After a tough negotiation, we signed an exclusive license agreement with USCI, granting it reasonable time to bring our technology onto the market after earning the applicable regulatory approvals. We expected that USCI, with its size and extensive worldwide distribution network and sales force, would successfully market products incorporating our technology.

What we did not anticipate was that USCI's real plan was to bury our invention in the large trash heap of other promising medical innovative technologies that would never come to fruition. Why? If USCI developed laser angioplasty it would cut into its own market share in the pre-laser, balloon angioplasty industry. Conservative USCI managers in New Jersey quietly decided that the competition was too risky. If they held the exclusive license to our technology, no competitor could ever license it from us. They also decided that if another company used the technology illegally, USCI would enforce our patents against that business, quashing the competition. USCI wanted to ensure that no patient would ever be treated with laser angioplasty.

This strategy for disposing of competing technologies turned out to be fairly common in the innovative medical products arena. Sometimes successful and even less costly medical-device technology falls prey to corporate avarice in this way.

For a couple of years, Art and I periodically visited USCI's labs in the Route 128 corridor outside Boston. USCI was supposed to be developing the embodiments for our laser energy innovations, for blood vessels. During our visits, USCI scientists put on a carefully orchestrated show in which they performed laser experiments at their lab benches. We saw equations on blackboards and other window dressing of supposed developmental significance. Our time there was carefully controlled, and our contact with the scientists was filled with carefully planned obfuscation. They strung us along for as long as they could, knowing that we could not license the technology to another company. So long as we were placated and hoped to see large financial gains, USCI could use our patents to prevent potential rivals from developing our technology and keep competition out of the market.

However, our agreement with USCI/Bard called for discernible milestones to be met by certain times, or the license would lose its exclusivity. Art and I, in talks with our consultants, finally decided after a couple of years that USCI was up to no good. We were shocked that someone would go to all this trouble to ensure that a promising new technology would never enter the market. We had little choice but to conclude that we had been duped.

We sued USCI when it became obvious that we were getting the run-around on development. The lawsuit caused them to back off and relinquish their exclusivity and their stranglehold on the technology. They realized that they could not defend what they were up to, and they settled our claim. Shortly thereafter, U.S. regulators and prosecutors cut USCI out of the lucrative balloon angioplasty market because of the company's unrelated criminal activities. Fortunately, we did not go down with it.

This late 1980s courtroom battle against USCI was the beginning of decades of life-changing events for me, an emotional roller coaster that brought me tragedy as well as insight into societal and other human problems.

Once the USCI issue was resolved, Art and I were free to license our technology non-exclusively for other medical purposes, such as laser kidney stone removal and the partial removal of enlarged prostates in older men. But laser angioplasty, the removal or evaporation of arteriosclerotic plaque blocking various crucial arteries, was the true prize for us and the public. The thought of eliminating much heart bypass surgery and being more effective than balloon angioplasty, was exciting.

CHAPTER 3

LAIS had infringed our hard- earned patents, and we were on a collision course. The newly public company was flush with tens of millions of dollars raised on the NASDAQ. Its investors probably expected those funds to go for development, clinical testing, manufacturing and sales of life- saving medical technology -- and not necessarily for battling over frivolous legal matters the company engendered. If the lawsuit turned out badly for LAIS, it would have to answer for it to the investors.

We sued LAIS for patent infringement. In a counterclaim, LAIS asked the federal court to invalidate our U.S. patents and also tried to prove that its products did not infringe the patents. That type of tit-for-tat game is commonly played in patent infringement cases.

LAIS refused to compromise, and both sides bet everything on the outcome. This was LAIS's choice. We had none.

The caution, experience and more impersonal style that might characterize a larger, established medical innovation company that really wanted to develop and sell a new medical technology, was lacking at LAIS. Like many start-ups, it was run by slick, fast- talking entrepreneurs with a get- rich-quick mentality who took everything personally. LAIS should have had a more studied approach that might have resulted in a settlement of the dispute without expensive and risky litigation and with a reasonable royalty license for us. But with their giant egos, LAIS's managers felt invincible and saw us as two puny interlopers. The stakes were high, and the dice had been rolled. LAIS was confident that it would crush Art and me.

LAIS intended to show in court that the United States Patent and Trademark Office had erred in granting our strong and broad patent claims because there was "prior art" in the public domain by the time of our first patent applications nearly ten years earlier. That is, LAIS would try to prove that the wherewithal to make our technology was already publicly known when we did our research and filed for the applications.

Secondly, the Southern California company planned to provide evidence that its laser angioplasty instruments were different from what our patent claims taught and so not governed by them. That is to say, they did not infringe our patent claims. Thirdly, LAIS needed to demonstrate that we inventors or our patent lawyers had defrauded the [U.S.] Patent and Trademark Office and held back information that might have caused it to reject our patent application. This latter theory is peculiarly American and forces the patent applicants/owners to defend themselves. It also ensures there will be mudslinging during the trial.

The prize for LAIS, if it succeeded in any of those legal strategies, would have been an extra five or ten percent profit on what promised to become a major medical technological advancement. From what we usually saw on audits of company royalty reports, the profit margins on sales of these types of products were well over 100% of the operating costs for making and selling them.

LAIS committed six to eight million dollars to this legal battle. The company's cocky management team appeared not to have seriously considered the possibility of losing.

Art and I knew early on that one day we might have to

defend our invention in court, and we dreaded the prospect. The time had come, and we scraped together the best team we could find to fight for our rights. Patents do not enforce themselves, and the rare patentees who are individuals and not large companies are on their own. Some have suggested that intentional patent infringement should be criminalized. It is not so now, merely a civil violation which makes it far too easy for companies to do what LAIS did: infringe, and if worse comes to worse, pay later. There is pitifully little incentive for them to follow the law and do the right thing.

The historical odds against this type of investment are very long. Individual patent owners do not usually win patent infringement lawsuits. Not only are these lawsuits extremely expensive for an individual to bring, but the inventing and patenting effort to get to that point is also very costly and time-consuming.

Judge Bryan entered the courtroom at ten sharp, and the show started. First, we had to pick jurors. In those days, as technical as things would become in patent infringement cases, juries comprised of ordinary citizens from the voting rolls, were charged with making the findings of fact. Nowadays some of what used to be decided by the jury is determined only by the judge.

The facts the jurors had to decide in patent validity and infringement cases like ours were complex scientific and medical concepts. The jurors were also responsible for deciding whether we or our lawyers had committed fraud during the Patent and Trademark Office application process.

Once the twelve carefully selected finders of fact were seated in Judge Bryan's jury box, counter-plaintiff LAIS went first, alleging grave miscarriages of patent issuance. The company also insisted that our claims of patent infringement were wild and frivolous.

LAIS had forty-one patent lawyers from three major U.S.

firms working on the case, but their lead attorney was a criminal lawyer, John Lowe of Washington, D.C. LAIS's strategy was first to present facts about science and technology, patent validity and infringement and the law. If that failed, LAIS would paint our patent lawyer, George Myers, and me as crooks who had set out to defraud the Patent and Trademark Office when we applied for patents and successfully appealed its initial decisions against us.

LAIS hoped to persuade the jury that we were despicable people guilty of patent fraud, known in legal parlance as inequitable conduct.

In addition to its forty-two lawyers, LAIS had packed the small courtroom with dozens of potential adverse expert and fact witnesses. Judge Bryan quickly cut that number to a handful to avoid duplication. On the patent invalidity issue, involving optics, light and laser energy, LAIS entrusted its case largely to a well known dermatologist and laser researcher from the Massachusetts Institute of Technology and Harvard. The company's expert witnesses all commanded a very high fee.

For about three hours, the jury was treated to polished testimony from this articulate opposing expert. When our turn came, our main patent litigator, Jeff Schwab, cross-examined the witness. He was assisted by Dr. Bob Gammon, our scientific expert, who sat at the counsel table throughout the trial.

Schwab asked the opposing expert: "Doctor, wasn't all of your work and published research on laser reactions in and beneath the skin?"

Witness: "Yes, but it would be the same for the muscle layer inside the heart vessels."

Schwab held up some journals before the witness and in view of the jury. "Then, how is it that you describe in several of your publications, in talking about your own laser inventions, the uniqueness of the differential absorption of certain laser energies by the various pigmented layers in the dermis of the skin?"

In the end, Schwab palpably shook this expert witness' credibility by exposing inconsistencies between his written words and his testimony. When it came to laser- tissue inter- actions inside blood vessels, the eminent dermatologist had no experience.

I hoped that this would not be lost on the twelve people in the jury box. From time to time, I glanced in their direction to try to fathom how they were reacting. I tried to be discreet and respectful toward them, even though I was terrified. I had never been in such a situation before and had no idea how it would end.

LAIS's next witness was an eccentric-looking older sci- entist from Duke University who asserted that the company's products did not infringe our patents' claims. He had dabbled in some optical- related research, much of which I considered significantly outside the mainstream. His name was well known in certain academic circles for other work he had done, and he had been a prolific author in his field. He laid out seem- ingly strong arguments for non- infringement as well as for the invalidity of our patents. Then our side got a chance to cross- examine him.

Schwab: "Doctor, you aren't a physician, but a Ph.D., cor- rect?"

Witness: "True, but I have done a lot of work on optics, involving the discipline of Ophthalmology, and the patents in question concern optics."

Schwab: "So, it's true that you haven't used the LAIS devices yourself?"

Witness: "Yes, but light is light."

Schwab: "You haven't even seen the LAIS machines, have

you?"

Witness: "That doesn't matter, I know how their optics work. I read all their manuals."

Schwab: "The LAIS instruments are used in very small vessels, in body lumens, in which laser light energy can spread to the surrounding environment easily. Would you agree?"

Witness: "My investigations and publications show that that isn't so within the eye.

Schwab: "But the eye is not a body lumen, and the heat absorption phenomena there are, in fact, very different from those within small lumens, like small blood vessels, aren't they?"

Witness: "I am quite happy with the results of my published work on laser effects in eyes, and I know it has been well received generally."

Schwab had been prepared for his line of questioning by our cardiologist- expert, who had used the LAIS machines and studied how they worked. We knew that the LAIS expert could not relate his own work to the use of the defendant company's laser instruments in patients and that his testimony was vulnerable to being rendered ineffective. He was also definitely not authoritative on the science related to our patents' and claims' validity and what distinguished them from prior relevant medical and scientific publications.

Junk science can sound compelling, but its basic factual assumptions are fundamentally flawed. An articulate witness or a highly regarded publication may be sufficient to persuade a jury that junk science is right. I hoped our jury would be able to distinguish fact from erudite- sounding fiction.

LAIS presented its piece de resistance, a so-called inequitable conduct witness: a retired, longtime United States Patent and Trademark Office lawyer, who attacked George Myers, our patent attorney.

Schwab cross- examined the witness. "You were already retired, sir, when the Fox patents were before the United States Patent and Trademark Office, weren't you?"

Witness: "Yes, but for this case I read several thousand pages of Patent Office files and all of the history there of these patents. I'm quite certain I learned everything there is to know about them."

Schwab: "You have determined, if I understand your prior testimony here in this courtroom, that Mr. George Myers had information that he got from Dr. Fox that he then withheld from the Patent Office in his prosecution of these patents there, is that correct?"

Witness: "Absolutely. During my long career with the Patent Office, I learned how to smell inequitable conduct from half a mile away. This is a classic and grotesque case of that kind of fraud."

Schwab: "What, specifically, is the essence of the material that you believe was relevant and was withheld from the Patent Office?"

Witness: "It is material about relevant scientific principles, written by the expert witness who testified before I did, material he had occasion to send to Dr. Kenneth Fox."

A copy of the written material was produced, and a short recess was called, so that our side could study it.

When the trial resumed, Schwab continued cross-examining the retired Patent Office lawyer: "Who gave you a copy of this material?"

The retired lawyer pointed to the previous witness, who was sitting in the courtroom gallery. "The author himself gave it to me to review for this case."

Schwab: "How do you know this was sent to Dr. Fox and that he received it?"

Witness: "I was assured of that by the author when he

sent me the material."

Schwab: "Doesn't this writing have to do with optics and the eye?"

Witness: "Yes."

Schwab: "Does it appear to mention body lumens, blood vessels and other things related to the substance and the claims of the Fox patents?"

Witness: "Well, I really don't know, I am not an expert on that subject."

Schwab: "When was this material written, sir?"

Witness: "In 1984, I understand. It doesn't appear to have a date."

Schwab: "When did Mr. Myers submit the Fox patents to the Patent Office?"

Witness: "I don't recall that date off the top of my head."

Schwab asked Judge Bryan to allow the witness to look at his voluminous material to ascertain the date that Myers submitted the Fox patents to the Patent Office.

Schwab continued: "I repeat, when was that submission to the Patent Office, sir?"

Witness: "Apparently, it was in March 1983."

Schwab: "Turning to another matter, sir, do you happen to know juror number seven in the jury box, the older gentleman in the first row, on your right?"

Witness: "Now that you mention it, I believe I do."

Schwab: "How so?"

Witness: "That gentlemen is my next door neighbor."

Schwab: "Last evening, sir, did you knock on that gentleman's door?"

Witness: "Well, I did," he paused. "But, he had borrowed one of my garden tools a couple of weeks ago, and it occurred to me to get it back, that's all.

Schwab: "Well, sir, during an earlier recess today, that juror approached Judge Bryan, and in the attorneys' presence advised us of what happened and asked for guidance from the court. He said that he didn't know until he saw you in the courtroom today that you were connected with this case.

"By the way, have you and Mr. Lowe worked together before on other court cases?"

Witness: "Well, let me think. Yes, a few times."

Schwab: "Would you consider Mr. Lowe a personal friend?

Witness: "Not necessarily."

Schwab: "Have you been to his home, socially?"

Witness: "Yes, I think that may have happened once or twice.

Finally, it was criminal lawyer Lowe's grand finale. He called a surprise rebuttal witness, Dr. Steven Charles from Memphis, Tennessee. Dr. Charles had been carefully hidden by Lowe earlier that morning while he waited for his turn to be called to the witness stand.

Lowe: "Dr. Charles, what is your current position?"

Witness: "I am a clinical professor of ophthalmology at the University of Tennessee School of Medicine in Memphis, Tennessee, and I have a private practice there, too."

Lowe: "Dr. Charles, do you know Dr. Kenneth Fox, who is sitting over there?"

Witness: "Yes sir, I met him briefly about fifteen years ago in Memphis. He was working with a former colleague of mine, doing clinical work and research."

Lowe: "Did you form any opinions then about Dr. Fox?"

Witness: "Yes, I did. I didn't feel that he was a credible individual. I didn't like the paper he published from the work he did then. There may have been some other things, too."

Lowe: "As a result of what you know about Dr. Fox, do you have an opinion as to whether he would be likely to withhold relevant information from the Patent Office in order to favorably influence an application he might have submitted?"

Schwab: "Objection, your honor."

Judge: "Overruled. I'll allow his opinion on this for what it's worth. You may answer, doctor."

Witness: "Yes, I certainly do."

Lowe: "And what is that opinion, based upon your knowledge of Dr. Fox?"

Witness: "I believe he would lie."

There was a brief recess as our side huddled to determine how to deal with this witness.

Schwab, in cross-examination: "Dr. Charles, how did you get here from Memphis, Tennessee today?"

Witness: "I flew here."

Schwab: "On what airline did you fly?"

Witness: "My own. You see, I fly my own private jet. I'm a pilot, too."

Schwab: "And how is it that Mr. Lowe contacted you to ascertain your opinions vis-a-vis Dr. Kenneth Fox for this case?"

Witness: "He told me he had read some of my medical publications."

Schwab: "Oh, and by the way, the publication of Dr. Fox's that you mentioned, when did you read it? Did you read it when it was published about thirteen years ago?"

Witness: "Mr. Lowe sent it to me to read in preparation for this court appearance."

Schwab: "How is it that you didn't read Dr. Fox's publication back when it was published if you were so interested in aspects of what he had done and how he did them?"

Witness: "I normally don't have time to read much of what other people write since I'm a very busy surgeon and spend a lot of time writing my own articles."

Schwab: "Doctor, you said that you never worked with Dr. Fox, is that correct?"

Witness: "Yes, but I heard enough about him from my ex-partner."

Schwab: "If you weren't in court today testifying against Dr. Fox, what would you be doing?"

Witness: "I would be in surgery. I had to cancel fifteen cases, so I could fly here today to be in court."

Schwab: "Is Mr. Lowe paying you for your appearance today?"

Witness: "No, I volunteered so that the truth would come out. I'm interested in justice. I gave up more than thirty thousand dollars in surgical fees today just so I could be here."

Schwab: "How many surgical days a week like that do you generally have scheduled?"

Witness: "Two, maybe three."

Schwab: "Thank you for coming here today, Dr. Charles. I think we have heard quite enough from you already, and I have no further questions."

Charles's court appearance was the continuation of his professional vendetta against me from years earlier. Now that he had appeared as a purported key witness for LAIS's defense against our patent infringement claims, I was beginning to discern some suggestive body language from the jury box. I hoped that they had had enough of LAIS's bizarre approach to this patent infringement litigation and were unconvinced. It would be three more agonizing days before I could know for sure.

Next up was our side. First into the witness box, I testified at length about how we invented the technology and explained the technology as well as the patenting efforts and the clinical applications. When Lowe got his chance to cross-examine me, he attacked me personally. He ignored my extensive testimony, which should have been the substance of the case: the science, the use of the technology and the patenting process. Mr. Lowe had nothing to back up his malicious innuendo, but innuendo can be powerful.

I spent four long days imagining what the jurors were thinking. I desperately hoped they would sense that our side was diligent and serious and that LAIS's presentation bordered on the farcical.

In retrospect, I suppose the huge LAIS team expected me to crack under its pressure. I held my head high and withstood their abusive and slanderous attacks on my credibility and competence as well as I could. I tried to convince myself that this was the price of justice.

While I was on the witness stand, LAIS brought out a multitude of charts and diagrams that it had paid scientists, engineers, clinicians and artists to prepare for the jury. These allegedly showed inaccuracies, lies or deficiencies in our case. Judge Bryan disqualified them, one by one, after we objected that they were baseless. There was no substance, and Judge Bryan did not buy them.

Dr. Bob Gammon took the witness stand for our side and explained complex physics principles in a simple, engaging way. Lowe, a criminal lawyer who knew less about technical matters than most of his patent law colleagues in the courtroom, asked:

"Dr. Gammon, who are the acknowledged world's experts in the specific area of light interference about which you are testifying today?"

Gammon: "I wrote all of the original articles

published on that subject, sir."

With each of his answers to Lowe's questions, Gammon seemed to dig LAIS's grave deeper.

George Myers testified, essentially in his own defense, about fraud on the Patent Office. He was genuine and well prepared with every detail of our numerous and lengthy patent dealings. He seemed extraordinarily competent.

LAIS may have shot itself in the foot. With all its lawyers, LAIS was Goliath and we were David, at least it seemed to me. LAIS Chief Executive Officer and President Robert Wall sat at the company's counsel table for four days in ultra-expensive Armani suits, with an abundance of gold chains and a gold watch. Mr. Wall testified briefly for his side. When cross-examined by Schwab on how his company had developed its laser angioplasty medical equipment, Wall said:

"LAIS never heard of the Fox and Coster patents. And now that we have been dragged into this courtroom, we find them entirely unnecessary and irrelevant."

The company had hired a professional artist to sit in the public gallery and draw caricatures of Art, Gammon, Myers, Schwab and myself in demeaning poses. Wall and his cronies intended that after LAIS won, the drawings would be exhibited at company headquarters in Los Angeles.

The testimony ended late on Wednesday, and on Thursday, each side gave its closing arguments. When Judge Bryan gave his instructions to the impaneled jurors it became clear that LAIS's pretentious, duplicitous and rather curious exhibition had not been lost on him.

The judge decides on the wording of the questions that jurors must answer in order to reach their verdict. While both sides' lawyers argue about the wording of those questions, or juror interrogatories, the judge makes the final call. The precise wording of the interrogatories can make a significant difference in the jury's decision.

The jury deliberations were to begin at nine on Friday morning.

CHAPTER 4

Art had sat silently in court, never having testified. On Thursday evening, we left the courthouse. We were to meet again later that night at the law office, to do a post- mortem on the trial.

While walking to where his car was parked several blocks away, Art wandered through the lobby of the Holiday Inn in Old Town Alexandria, Virginia. On the hotel's Events of the Day board, he saw:

"8:30 p.m. (Madison Room)-- Advanced Interventional Systems Dinner and Victory Party."

Art 'was aghast. A few members of the opposing team were sitting in the lobby as he walked through on that cold autumn night. Out of the corner of his eye, he saw some of them glare at him and others smirk. Art told me an hour later about LAIS's pre-victory victory party. I wondered what they knew that we did not.

On Friday, the jurors did not take much more than an hour to reach a verdict. Every minute of waiting was agony. We did not know whether more than a dozen years of work with almost nothing to show for the effort was down the drain. We did not know whether the hundreds of thousands of dollars spent on the research, patenting, and litigation had come to nothing. If we won, we could continue, taking our work as far as we could imagine. If we lost, we were done. Invalid patents are not enforceable. Our fate was in the hands of twelve strangers.

The jury foreperson read the decisions for each of our many patent claims in question:

"Valid and infringed."

"Valid and infringed."

"Valid and infringed."

Those were the magic words that an inventor needs to hear. The jury also found that the inequitable conduct allegations were bogus. I felt like screaming with joy.

You should have seen the expressions on the faces of LAIS's executives and forty-two lawyers when the jury verdict was read. That was a picture to savor.

Later that day, the judge granted our post-trial motion for an injunction to prevent LAIS from making, selling or using their infringing products. This punishment is the patent holder's ultimate weapon. Since it covered all of LAIS's products, the start-up was out of business.

Obviously, we did not benefit from shutting down the distributor of our technology. Something had to be done.

On the following Monday, LAIS Chief Financial Officer Bing Crosby, not the old crooner but a stocky, cigar-chomping namesake, and a new LAIS legal team appeared in George Myers' offices ready to make a deal with Pillco. They had flown east over the weekend following the company's defeat in court. They had no choice. While they could appeal, they would not be able to produce or sell anything unless and until the Court of Appeals for the Federal Circuit decided the case in their favor, by reversing. It would probably have taken over a year for that court, which hears all patent appeals in the United States, to decide the case in their favor, if it were to do so. Also, it is extremely difficult to reverse a jury finding.

Their emergency attempts in Judge Bryan's trial court and

then across the Potomac River in Washington, D.C. at the Court of Appeals for the Federal Circuit to have Judge Bryan's injunction vacated were summarily dismissed the previous Friday afternoon. That left LAIS out in the cold.

So, LAIS took the only step it could take at that time. It was offered a non- exclusive forward royalty license in exchange for a pile of cash. That is what we wanted all along, and, finally, our hope was realized. Or so it seemed at that moment.

While the belated licensing maneuver saved Advanced Interventional Systems for a short while, the self-inflicted damage would prove to be fatal. LAIS sued its insurer, the St. Paul Insurance Company, to try to recover enough to offset the losses and expenses from the unnecessary but costly litigation against Pillco. That attempt failed.

LAIS's shareholders hit the company with a class-action lawsuit for mismanagement of our patents and the licensing. After the company lost that one, it had taken too many body blows to continue. CEO Wall was already long gone. LAIS's only option was to merge with its competitor in laser angioplasty technology, Spectranetics Corporation, another start-up.

Inventing innovative medical technology had become a passion for me. I am proud that many people in many countries have benefited from our technology. In the beginning, I thought that if we had excellent technology, did our homework and were lucky, we could provide a crucial medical device to doctors. Inventing can be a long, lonely, uncertain, unappreciated and often anonymous process. Once in a while, it leads to a meaningful discovery that is commercialized and makes a difference. If I had known the odds against it succeeding, I might never have taken on the challenge in the first place.

All medical technology companies desperately need excellent technology protected by patents. And, they need replacement technology since the half- life of the newest innovations is not that long. Something else comes along, better and/or cheaper, or the patents expire. These key factors force innovative medical device companies to continue to fill their pipelines with new technologies, just like pharmaceutical companies need new medicines. Without something new to offer in a timely fashion, they will not survive.

When manufacturers agree to pay a fair royalty to the inventors or patent holders to use their technology, everyone benefits. The inventor is fairly paid for long and arduous efforts. The manufacturing/distributing company, the patent licensee, can better compete with the latest and best technologies in a tough but potentially profitable business environment.

The health industry comprises about 15 percent of gross domestic product worldwide. This includes health care as well as biotechnology, pharmaceuticals and medical devices, although they are increasingly tied together because of mergers and acquisitions and vertical and horizontal integration. More companies are large and multinational.

Eleven years or so after the LAIS trial in Alexandria, Virginia, I developed and taught a course in the Management of Innovative Medical Technology for a Masters in Business Administration (MBA) program. A lot of that course was drawn from my experience during the preceding twenty years of inventing and science, patenting, licensing, devising and implementing exit strategies, marketing, managing medical reimbursement, applying for government approvals for new drugs or medical devices and learning manufacturing practices and other aspects of medical products management.

I also drew upon my graduate business education in the Washington, D.C. area in the early 1980s. I studied business about a dozen years after I had graduated from medical school and completed five years of post- graduate training in Ophthalmology.

CHAPTER 5

At the time of the victory against LAIS, we also licensed the patents to Spectranetics. We did not have to sue Spectranetics for infringement since the specter of what had transpired in court was enough to keep the Colorado-based company in line.

However, by 1995, Spectranetics had already defaulted on some patent royalty payments and had played fast and loose on a number of patent licensing matters. We sued it for contract breach. Then Spectranetics paid; it had no serious defense.

Spectranetics, like many other start-up medical technology companies, had relatively inexperienced management. Spectranetics often had to compete with larger, better-funded companies, and its management seemed to sometimes suffer from paranoia and at other times from hyper-inflated egos.

By 1995, the time of our fourth patent-related lawsuit, this one against Spectranetics, Pillco had become quite successful.

After the LAIS case, Pillco licensed over a dozen medical device manufacturers around the world: two for interventions that were vascular, inside vessels, and the rest for lasers that removed kidney stones. The vascular interventions were the bulk of this business because of the huge volume of sales of individual disposable catheters for each patient. Our lithotripsy units also used lasers to remove kidney stones, but those devices did not employ disposable catheters. Each laser unit was pricey but still less expensive than those required for laser angioplasty, sometimes called laser atherectomy. Our kidney stone removal devices became prevalent around the world. The royalties depended on the number of the licensed items sold, so the laser angioplasty was, by far, the more lucrative for Pillco given all of those disposable catheter sales and attendant royalties.

The licensed companies included all the manufacturers making or experimenting with products that would require our patented technology for their laser systems. In the United States, royalties do not have to be paid during the experimental stages before regulatory approval. Still, manufacturers may be licensed expectantly at that early stage. Our patent lawyer, George Myers, and I frequently met with the president or CEO of a medical device company and sometimes also with its lawyers.

These deals were difficult, in part because a manufacturer only begrudgingly licenses patented technology it needs and because it always wants a deal at least as good as its competitors'. These deals were Pillco's only source of revenue, since Pillco did not manufacture. The patents were our lifeblood.

Three years after our victory against LAIS, Pillco had brought in more than five million dollars in royalties. There were thousands of licensed lasers using Pillco technology, each of them displaying my patents' registration numbers. Millions of patients around the world had been treated. Tens of thousands of lives had been saved with the vascular application.

Art and I had the benefit of some terrific local scientists with international reputations. We found Dr. Bob Gammon because Art had treated the physicist's mother. We signed a contract with him to consult for us.

Art and I had begun to work on other problems. Identifying the clinical issues that might be treated with innovative laser energy was my job. Art researched the background of the pathology we were targeting and did some other basic science research for us. We did some preliminary laser energy experiments. I used lasers from my clinical practice, and they provided the raw energy source for our experiments. But we also managed to hook up with sophisticated laser laboratories at the University of Maryland, College Park, Maryland and the Naval Research Laboratories in Washington, D.C.

Getting useful specimens for our direct laser energy experimental blasts was not easy. I was in touch with coroners' offices around the United States where the staff were kind enough to send us by Federal Express, cadaver vessels with arteriosclerotic plaques and other matter for our work. I also became familiar with people at local abattoirs who would provide animal tissue specimens for our research.

One big city coroner called me a grave robber when I described our experiments and begged for specimens from his morgue for use in a long planned laser laboratory experiment at the University of Maryland. Others were more accommodating. One coroner sent cadaver vessels packed on ice from San Francisco to Washington via Fedex. Unfortunately, the courier company lost the parcel in the bowels of its Springfield, Virginia warehouse just before the weekend. That calamity delayed our experiment for three months.

I lived for the eureka moments. Looking under a microscope and seeing how strong laser energy could be used to ablate arteriosclerotic plaque without damaging the normal surrounding blood vessel wall was a thrill. We tried to analyze how and why that happened. When you are breaking new ground, there is no one who can completely guide you.

By the 1990s, Art and I were applying some of the ultra-fast pulsed laser energy we had used for the vessel, kidney stone and related applications to eye surgery, my field. This was different because it was not deep inside the human body, but at the surface. Catheters were not needed as was the case to transmit that laser energy deep inside the body. There were greatly differing heat dissipation phenomena at play because the eye is much larger in diameter than the tiny vessels supplying the heart and brain.

We had begun to make significant inroads into discerning what type of laser energy parameters were best for impacting both the cornea, the clear part in the front of the eye, and the cloudy cataractous lens just inside the eye. That technology was not used on patients until about ten years later. Our work was seminal when we did it, but was surpassed later after events halted our investigations. The technology was ultimately used for laser incisions for cataract or corneal transplant surgery and for removing the cataractous lens itself.

So much seems to depend on so little. My fate may be determined by one juror's vote, one judge's decision, one word in a patent application. The course of my life may depend on finding a replacement law firm that will work on a contingency basis in an emergency.

There was no way that Art and I could have paid the millions of dollars required for the patent legal battles against well-funded opponents seeking to drive us out of existence. We had to have contingency fee arrangements where we did not pay expenses, but the law firm shared handsomely in the royalties we would receive if we were successful. At least once, our lawyers quit in the middle of a patent trial for reasons we never really knew. I suspected that something sinister had happened at that patent law firm in Alexandria, Virginia in 1991. Fortunately and against all expectations, the court gave us a few extra months to find new lawyers before the trial.

Sometimes one little thing can make a monumental difference. The mutation of just one gene can drastically change a personality. A small arteriosclerotic plaque in a small vessel can kill. A small tear in the far corner of a retina can lead to blindness. How the genetic mutation affected my life will become clear later. My invention could treat the plaque, and my clinical career focused on the surgical treatment of retinal tears and their consequences.

One unforeseen occurrence that changed my life happened

in 1988, nearly a decade after we applied for our earliest patents. We ultimately obtained more than a dozen patents in the United States, Canada, the European Union, South Korea, Japan and Australia, but at that time we were still trying to get that first one, issued in the United States.

We had been rejected by the United States Patent and Trademark Office at first, and I thought all was lost. This was before the patent licensing could begin in earnest, before the commercialization of the technology.

George Myers was preparing to attend the Patent and Trademark Office Appeals Board hearing in Arlington, Virginia. I asked to join him. He agreed but warned me that only the lawyers may participate and not the patent applicants.

During the conversation between the three appellate patent board members and Myers, there was an impasse over how Art and I knew about an aspect of our technology at a certain point in time. The issue was whether we could have known without having had access to certain alleged prior art -- earlier publications of scientific literature or similar documents.

I instinctively blurted out, "I think I can explain that." Surprisingly, the board members allowed me to speak. I spent the next fifteen minutes explaining some fairly intricate steps in our investigations that led to the deduction that explained our knowledge at that time, as stated in the patent application. They were impressed. The Board reversed the examiner and granted our first U.S. patent.

CHAPTER 6

Getting into medical and scientific research had not been part of my plan.

I was a clinician, that is, a doctor who treated patients. I had years of specialized training in medical school, an internship and an Ophthalmology residency and subspecialization fellowship training in retinal and vitreous diseases and surgery. The eye is only about an inch, or two and half centimeters, long, so a specialty in it is highly focused, pardon the pun.

I first started doing clinical research for large medical products makers. I tested new products geared for Food and Drug Administration approval in the United States and other countries. I wrote and participated in dozens of peer- reviewed papers for years, stemming from my clinical work and my clinical research.

But getting involved in pulsed laser energy research was a fluke.

After Art approached me at the hospital that one evening, we started experimenting and quickly got hooked. There was always more testing to do. The research took a lot of time, energy and money. All effort, no reward, until much later. But nothing stays the same, and very little is predictable. I had to be flexible.

Medical school and residency were not easy for me. For a few people, they may seem like a breeze, but for me, they were a challenge. There is a lot to learn and practice, and I was serious and dedicated. I had a flair for eye surgery, and I enjoyed interacting with patients.

I had the good fortune to practice medicine in six countries on four continents. I worked with indigent inner city residents and affluent suburbanites. I volunteered in public clinics and hospitals and went on medical missions to rural places in Latin America, Asia, the Caribbean and Africa on behalf of a charity. I also worked in tertiary care -- academic and referral settings -- with patients aged one to one hundred.

Once I got into private practice, I wanted to thrive in it, but that road was littered with potholes and, in some instances, damn near impassable conditions.

When I started to subspecialize in retinal and related diseases and surgery, and was close to achieving my original career goal, lightning struck.

I went to train with a retinal surgeon. I interviewed with David at his large practice and spoke with others who had been there before, including a recent associate of his. I was warned against working with him. Foolishly, I ignored this advice, perhaps because the field was so competitive and the choices were few. Maybe I was too young and inexperienced to know better.

After I went to work there, I realized that David was probably a manic depressive. Manic depressives can be dangerous. When they are not in the right mood, they can be unpredictable and irresponsible. Some people who suffer from manic depression, or bipolar disorder, may be controlled and some manage to get by. But, in general, getting an individual with bipolar disorder, as a patient, to agree to treatment and continue it is difficult. I knew nothing about that in those days, and it nearly ruined my career before it even started.

Nearly everyone found this mentor of mine impossible to work with. Almost from the very beginning of the fellowship, he refused to provide the teaching and training he had promised. At the last minute, another guy came along whom he saw as a future associate in his practice, a replacement for the one he had just lost when that professional relationship went sour. David then stopped paying me. I wound up doing clinical research using practice and hospital medical records but rarely saw patients after the first few months. Being around David was downright scary.

To make matters worse, just when I arrived so did Charles, for a new association that David had planned earlier. Charles was the surprise witness against me at the trial sixteen years later. He was an egomaniac and decided to bear a grudge against me forever although I never even worked with him. Later, adversaries of mine in Washington, D.C. fed him lies about me.

They fueled his fire, but that did not take much. At that time, he arrived as another new associate in that retinal practice, but their association did not last long.

Once my sentence with David was up, I headed to London for the better part of a year at the world-renowned Moorfield's Eye Hospital, affiliated with the University of London, to train with more than a dozen expert eye surgeons and other physicians in retina and vitreous. I gained valuable experience that held me in good stead later.

In the later 1970s, training finally completed, I returned to the Washington, D.C. area where I had gone to medical school at Georgetown. I opened an Ophthalmology practice. Striking out on my own, without connections, was always going to be difficult, particularly in highly competitive suburban Washington. The region was already crawling with a few hundred Ophthalmologists. Joining another doctor or a group practice sometimes can make entry into the market easier. Today, it is nearly impossible to go it alone.

I have always been fiercely independent. I believed that I if I trained hard and committed myself, I could accomplish my goal. I am allergic to failure. I have learned, sometimes with great pain, that there is often no substitute for perseverance. Sometimes it is very hard to keep going. There are probably both good and bad things about that trait.

By the mid-1980s I had established a successful private practice in the Washington area. I had built the first free- standing eye clinic in the area, called the Atlantic Eye Center. I was chairman of Ophthalmology at the hospital where I met Art. I started a company called Intherea that did clinical research for pharmaceutical companies, and I brought on board other eye clinics around the United States, providing multiple testing sites for our pharmaceutical clients' U.S. clinical trials.

Because of my practice and published articles in peer- reviewed Ophthalmology journals, I was often asked to review medical law cases, including some Ophthalmology malpractice claims. I set up another company called Ophthalmology Associates for reviewing cases either opposing or defending other ophthalmic surgeons from around the country. Ophthalmology Associates grew substantially, and I brought in other expert Ophthalmologists to help review cases for attorneys.

Despite the rumors that my adversaries were spreading, the vast majority of claims I reviewed favored the defendant or would-be defendant Ophthalmologist. In return for a fair fee for my time, I reviewed the medical records presented to me by my client lawyers. I often succeeded in persuading the plaintiff's attorneys not to sue or to drop the claims against the doctor. Occasionally I testified, and I became quite good at explaining complex clinical and scientific issues to jurors.

The secret to successful teaching is making the subject fun and interesting. I learned this in my early 20s when I was a first-grade teacher in New York City's Bedford-Stuyvesant ghetto before I went to medical school. That experience helped shape my character, making me more responsible and better at relating to others.

Some of my local Ophthalmology competitors hated me for opening the first independent eye clinic and surgery complex in the area, for being an expert witness and for doing clinical research. They hated the competition, and some of them ganged up on me. Not all of them were like that; many fellow ophthalmologists were also quite supportive, and many referred retinal patients to me. But a few of the malicious ones were powerful and ruthless. They became chairpeople of hospital committees, advisers to medical boards, advisers to local medical regulators and national medical specialty societies. Those were the people who got their names out, got the official nods, controlled the hospitals, societies and the regulatory bodies, or anyhow did so in disproportionate numbers.

Politics was a way for them to get and stay ahead. Sometimes they were more successful in medical politics than in clinical practice.

The rest of us were just trying to practice medicine. I was naive about these things in those days. I hoped I could be independent, do my best and be there for my patients. Medical and surgical ability, staying abreast of leading trends in a specialty, rapport with patients-- these are the things that should really make a difference, and these are what patients and the insurers who pay the bills should value the most.

It turned out that who you knew and who you kowtowed to was actually what mattered most. If you did not kiss up to them, you were marked an enemy. Some of "them" were also good doctors, but that was not necessarily what got them where they were or kept them where they were determined to stay. Medicine is no better than other competitive fields in this regard; those who are not part of the "in group" may be bullied and stabbed in the back. The more that is at stake, the worse it is.

That group, led by a few insiders, riled up Charles against me from a local hospital they controlled. Writing a bogus letter about me was as much of a high for him as flying his own Piper to Washington to testify in court against me. My self-appointed enemies made all sorts of wild charges and claims, none of which were remotely true, just to try to eliminate some of their competition. I was far from the only one in the field who has suffered this. In my case, the "insiders" got one guy to rummage through my patients' medical records at the hospital where I was the chief of Ophthalmology. They hired someone to contact patients on whom I had operated to try to convince them that I had maltreated them and that they should file a medical malpractice claim against me.

There were some local lawyers recommended by this in-group, who were standing by, ready to oblige those patients abused in this way by these guys. I hated working with that type of lawyer when I was an expert witness. Fortunately, most lawyers are not willing to stoop so low.

Another of my local politician-doctor adversaries, a self-anointed would- be authority figure for the specialty, organized fake complaints to the state medical board about me and others. I had to hire expert Ophthalmologists from around the United States to review the dozens of patient medical records in question and file reports to the board, to exonerate myself.

One complaint filed anonymously with a state regulator of hospitals claimed spuriously that my clinic was actually an improperly licensed hospital and should be shut down. The depths to which they would sink had no bounds.

I had to retain almost full time, a lawyer whose practice consisted of defending doctors against these intra-professional battles. A lot of my time was wasted defending myself against false claims, and it cost me a small fortune.

Patients do not benefit from their doctors fighting each other and trying to destroy rival practices. That is hardly better than medical device companies conspiring to keep the best technology off the market. These wars contributed to increases in health insurance premiums and medical costs. Medical malpractice claims raise doctors' negligence insurance premiums, and the costs are passed on to the patients or their insurers. That is also true of any increased expense for doctors.

There are legitimate reasons for taking a doctor to task. But for each doctor needing remediation, ten suffer unnecessarily, and their practices may be destroyed in the process. Lay people have no surefire way to determine what is legitimate medical care and what is phony; it is often quite opaque. In urban areas, there are too many competing physicians, and this is the unfortunate consequence.

I thought when I went into Medicine that my only bosses would be my patients. It turned out otherwise. I wound up with others trying to control everything I did-- and none of that was ever for any patient's benefit. My will to go on and my financial resources were strained by this, time and again.

By the mid-1980s, eight years into my practice and a dozen years into my career, I was pulled in many directions-- by my clinical practice, then still very strong, by the innovation business and by other things that will soon become clear.

I thought things were generally good, and I remained optimistic. I had a lot of friends. Wendy and I had been married in 1975 near the end of my medical training, and she had been as strong as a rock. In 1980, we had a daughter, and, three years later, a son. One of my long-time employees said to me: "Ken, you have the million-dollar family-- and life." In the 1980s, I thought she was right.

CHAPTER 7

It was about a quarter to six in the evening, and a Thursday, and I was working late in my medical office in suburban Washington. The private line rang.

"Ken?" my mother asked. Her voice sounded different. She'd never called me at the office before.

"Mom, how are you?"

"Okay. Can you come to New York tomorrow morning?" she replied.

Mom and Dad had lived in the same apartment in New York City for more than thirty-five years. Dad was sixty seven, and he still had his dental practice. I thought he was pretty healthy.

Mom, sixty three, had been teaching elementary school for twenty years. She became a teacher when my younger brother, Bob, went to high school. Mom was fine now, but seven years earlier she had the scare of her life when she was diagnosed with breast cancer. She had a mastectomy and was assured that "they got it all." She resumed all of her activities, including teaching, which she loved, and put that ugly episode behind her.

That is what went through my mind when I heard this unusual request from my mother. Mom would never presume that I could or should drop everything and come to New York to visit.

"What is it Mom? What's wrong?"

"Probably nothing, but I need you to help me make sure and figure it out."

"How is Dad," I thought next to ask.

"OK", she said resignedly . "Can you fly up on the shuttle as early in the morning as possible, and I'll explain when I see you?"

"OK. Should I tell you which shuttle it will be, so Dad or you can pick me up at La Guardia?" That was always the way it had worked when I flew to New York City to meet my parents. "No, just take a taxi, and I'll pay for it." It was hardly the taxi fare that bothered me. Something was very wrong.

I called Joan, my office manager, and tried to make the best arrangements I could to handle the patients I was supposed to see on Friday. When I got home, I told my wife and she made alternative arrangements for the family for what, I supposed, might be the weekend.

On Friday morning, the taxi brought me to the apartment in Forest Hills, the neighborhood of New York City where I had grown up and where my parents still lived. My mother was quick to answer the doorbell. She hugged me and asked me to come into the living room. It was just the two of us.

"I went to the doctor yesterday, the oncologist," Mom volunteered immediately. She almost choked on that last word. I began to think that I knew what this was all about, and I had a disgustingly sick feeling in my stomach.

"He told me that the cancer has come back. One of the bone scans he routinely did was positive, and they think there are some cancer cells in my spine." As a physician, I knew what this meant. It was probably too late to stop the cancer. I was barely able to keep from vomiting. I tried to keep from revealing my horror to my mother.

My mother and I just hugged for several minutes, and no other words were spoken.

"What does he recommend?" I eventually asked.

"Radiation and chemo, and we'll see." Her voice dropped off at the end of that utterance. That seemed to be all Mom had internalized and all she could deal with about this medical problem at the moment. "I asked him, even pleaded, to wait until the end of the school year in about six weeks, but he said it was too urgent to wait. So, I have to get it over with, and then see about things."

Mom was crying on the inside but trying hard not to let it show. My mother was a very tough person, incredibly strong, and I had gotten some of that from her. So this was very uncharacteristic, explained only by the extreme circumstances.

Almost as an afterthought, I asked, "Where is Dad?" I had instinctively arisen from the sofa at that moment, as if Dad would appear at the doorway. Whenever I arrived from out of town, both parents were always there to greet me. This time, it was only Mom.

'Well, that's the problem." I sank back down in the seat I had just left. If "that" was the problem, I knew we were in trouble, because I had thought I had just heard about "the problem."

"He's in the bedroom," Mom said. Thinking that he had just died, I slowly got up to see for myself.

"Wait," she said. "Let me tell you what happened. One night a couple of weeks ago, your father was very late coming home from the office. When he arrived, he was covered with dirt and mud. He told me he wasn't entirely sure what had happened except that the car had gotten stuck on the highway and he had to walk the last mile home.

"He's been confused ever since. I thought maybe he had had a stroke. He wouldn't let me call an ambulance or a doctor. You know your father-- he wouldn't see a doctor if he were dying." The thought then in my mind at this moment was that maybe he was. "Since then, he has been in and out of the house, even to the office," my mother continued. "I don't know how he sees patients in this state."

"Why didn't you call me earlier," I asked.

"He forbade me from doing it. He said to me 'I'm fine, I'm feeling better.' But I was fit to be tied. I just didn't know what to do about him."

"Oh my God." I got up, walked down the hallway toward the bedroom and opened the door, not knowing what I might find in there.

Dad was sitting in his recliner, in his underwear. The TV was on, but he looked just about asleep.

He heard the door and turned very slowly and hesitatingly towards me and managed a smile. But it was a kind of empty smile that strongly suggests that the one who is smiling has not the slightest clue as to why he is doing it.

"Kenny. I thought you might be coming; good to see you." Even the words did not come out without a bit of a hiccup. I almost felt like he had made a lucky guess when he called me by my name.

My father was obviously out of it. Normally, he was extremely mentally sharp, like my mother. The man I saw that morning was confused, slow in thinking and moving and very unsteady. Something was going on, and we were heading for a crossroads from which there was no turning back.

I hugged my father. I was trying to be strong in the face of what I just had seen and heard. It had to be a bad dream. I hoped that I would wake up and this nightmare would be over. But that never happened.

By 11:00 a.m., I was calling Bob at his medical office in Philadelphia. Mom had told me that no one else knew.

"Hi, Ken, what's up," my brother asked at the other end of the line.

"Sit down, and listen to me for a few minutes, and then we'll decide what to do," I replied, surmising my admonition would be sufficiently concerning to my brother.

Later that Friday, about 3:30 in the afternoon. Bob arrived

by car at the apartment. We had tentatively agreed between ourselves that Bob would take one parent, and I would take the other.

Prior to Bob's arrival, I had already called the dentist that my father leased space from and briefly explained the situation to him. He agreed that he would take over the care of the patients, and he even agreed to pay $1 for each medical record my father had. There were a lot of those since he had been in dental practice for over 40 years. I wrote out a short agreement, had my father sign it., and had a check from that guy in my hand within three days. I rightly surmised that my father's long dental career had just come to an abrupt end.

One problem solved. I also called the school, the principal, the Board of Education and the New York City teachers union that same day. I explained the situation, and they agreed to process the paperwork for my mother's now forced retirement, and her pension and annuity. Within about five weeks, she received all of it, although that part required a good bit more of my time and attention in the interim.

I also called their landlord. The company agreed to accept a couple weeks rent and short notice, and I paid by check -- so that phase was over. The landlord was delighted to get back a rent-controlled apartment in New York City. I called movers, arranged for them to come early the next week, pack everything in the apartment and put it in storage until I could determine what to do with it. I paid movers and arranged for an aunt living in New York to be there to supervise them. My aunt, who was grief- stricken by the news, also agreed to take care of a few matters with the phone company, the post office and so on.

I called my parents' banks and asked them to immediately send some forms that I anticipated my parents would need. My mother signed the papers, and funds were moved more conveniently for their benefit.

My mother attended to the packing of two bags, one for

each of them. They were about to be separated, hopefully for their ultimate good. I was not sure, then, if that was to be for the last time. They had been married more than 40 years.

After Bob arrived at the apartment, he surveyed the situation. I could see a discernible paleness come over his face. I hardly would have expected otherwise. By around 5:30 that afternoon we were on the road, eight hours after I had arrived that morning.

Bob left in his car with Dad and his things. and I took Dad's car with Mom and her things. Bob arranged through a physician friend for Dad's immediate admission to a hospital near Philly, and for cardiology, neurology and endocrinology consultations. Dad was so out of it that he could not mount a challenge; otherwise, incredibly stubborn as he was, he would never have agreed to any of it.

I called a friend, then an oncologist he recommended, and an internist. By 10 that evening Mom was admitted to a hospital we selected in Washington. Around midnight, about eighteen hours after I had left, I returned home. As tired as I felt, I didn't sleep at all that night.

CHAPTER 8

Dad spent six weeks in the hospital and several more weeks in a convalescent facility, recovering. After a month of tests and not until I suggested it in a conversation with Bob, did the doctors fully test Dad's thyroid function. Then they discovered his nearly fatal thyrotoxicosis, or severe overacting thyroid gland. The good news was that this problem was fairly easy to control, as was the secondary heart failure that had occurred because of it. The worse news was that the neurologists discovered while

Dad was in the hospital that he was suffering from Parkinson's Disease.

Parkinson's is a chronic, debilitating disease that can affect movement of the lower legs, arms and face as well as muscles elsewhere, causing them to respond abnormally. In Parkinson's, some neurons, or nerve cells, die, and so they stop making dopamine, which is needed for proper nerve electrical conduction, and function of the brain. It is a physical, not a mental illness. There may be tremors that are uncontrollable, rigidity of the legs and arms, a lack of normal tone of facial muscles, slowness of movement and problems with balance. Walking, fine hand motor tasks, even speaking can be and often is affected in Parkinson's patients. However, if Parkinson's pro-gresses uncontrolled, its consequences can be fatal, ultimately involving respiratory muscles. There are treatments, medi-cines, some of which affect dopamine metabolism, that con-trol the symptoms but do not cure. A sufferer's condition may deteriorate for years before the disease finally kills, if it pro-gresses that far.

My mother remained in the hospital for about a month. She had innumerable cancer tests and then triple treatment with some of the poisons they give to try to kill the cancer cells wherever they may have wandered in the body, during the metastasis. That made her sick and caused her hair to fall out. She got a major dose of radiation in sev-eral bony areas where the cancer had spread. Mom had pain in a lot of places, but she never complained. My mother re-fused almost any pain reliever. She was desperately afraid of becoming addicted and said she did not need it. Sometimes she could not stop herself from grimacing with pain. She al-ways felt that the next round of radiation, even the chemo or the hormonal therapy, would somehow cure her.

Mom could hardly walk, even with a walker. She pre-ferred the cane to the walker; to her it represented less of the stigma of a disability. Often, she could barely move to find a position that was slightly less agonizingly painful. The cancer was already in her spine, in her leg bones and her chest wall. The chemo was useless. The radiation was helpful for comfort for a while. Then the disease broke out somewhere else. She went downhill for about two more years, although the doctors' prognosis did not give her nearly that long to live.

Mom refused to accept any help except that which she absolutely needed, such as assistance to get out of bed and go to the bathroom. Nurses came to bathe her, but she always wanted to be dressed and to look -- so she thought -- as if she were well. She was usually bedridden but sometimes was able to get into a chair. If she could get out, she wanted that, because she still had a strong zest for life. She never acted like she was going to die, even when she looked all the world like she might, and she never, ever talked like she would.

Mom was on the telephone almost constantly. She had no problem using her arms and hands, and her mind was in an excellent state throughout. She talked all the time to whomever she could. It was a kind of a lifeline for her. She would read all the while, never giving up that avid habit of hers. Her vision was fine. This would allow her to escape, and she loved it. When she could, she would knit or bead, things she was good at and loved. She could no longer do more strenuous activities. She compensated in amazing ways with so much inner strength that I never ceased to be astounded by her. Over the years, I do not believe I ever saw any of my own patients show as much of that kind of spirit. Being around family was a great stimulus for my mother. At the same time, she had to deal with guilt about being burdensome. Deterioration can be demeaning, and it weighs on the afflicted.

After about three or four months in Washington, Mom announced that it was time for her and my father to move into a place of their own, with their own furniture. She had been staying with us. Mom thought she and Dad should be together and resume as normal a life as possible.

For all of their married life, she had considered Dad to be impossible. Their relationship, so distressing when I was growing up, was a disaster. She reluctantly confided to me that if something happened to her, she really did not know how I would deal with my father. She felt that his stubbornness and orneriness would be overwhelming, and she would not be around to buffer it. I tried to disavow her of that concern, although privately I worried about that, too. That was the only time that my mother talked as if she knew she might die. Her greatest concern seemed to be that he would become a burden for me.

There came a time when my father was having trouble holding things without dropping them. Walking was becoming increasingly difficult for him. One evening approximately a year later, the three of us planned to go to a restaurant for dinner, part of that normalcy thing my mother craved.

My mother had recently had radiation and felt a little less in pain. She had dressed up that evening almost as if she were going to a ball. I was shocked when I arrived at their apartment, some twenty minutes from my house, and saw that my mother had jettisoned the flat, rubber- soled shoes with traction and had donned high heels for the occasion. At those times, even my father had acquiesced to wearing rubber -soled shoes with more traction.

"Mom, change those shoes now, please" I exhorted in my most demanding tone.

"No, Ken, I'm fine. No problem," she replied defiantly.

She had not even walked the ten meters from her bedroom to the living room before she hit the hardwood floor, crashing onto her knee. I have never before or since heard such a scream of agony!

In the emergency room, three quarters of an hour later,

we found out Mom had shattered her patella, the knee cap bone, in the fall. A normal person would not break a knee cap in a similar fall, but her patella had been laden with cancer cells and had pathologically fractured, a term that meant it disintegrated from the cancer that had invaded it. Mom never walked again.

My mother refused to go to a hospice. She wanted to stay at home, with as much extra help as was required but with as little of it as she could manage. She was acutely hospitalized five times over about two years, all for the cancer. This was in addition to dozens upon dozens of doctor's visits, radiation and chemotherapy. All of this took a significant toll on my life, on my father, and on all of us. The only light at the end of this otherwise dark tunnel of despair was the hope my mother exuded with her smiles and good words in the face of her personal tragedy.

About two years to the day from the time of the diagnosis of the breast-cancer recurrence, my mother was admitted to yet another area hospital. She languished there for almost two months, still making her phone calls, reading and enjoying visits by family members. Near the end, the cancer spread to her eighth cranial or acoustic nerve on one side, and she lost the hearing in that ear, as a result. The cancer had spread to her brain. So she shifted ears and continued talking on that phone almost until to the end.

As I wound up my visit one Tuesday evening, I told her, "Mom, I just want you to know that no one has a better mother than do I. I love you." Less than an hour after I got home that evening, a hospital nurse called, telling me that my mother had slipped into a coma. She died on the following Thursday morning in early July 1988.

Dad was disoriented for a short while after Mom died. We somehow managed to get him to the funeral and to the burial site.

My mother died ultimately from pneumonia, which her doctors did not treat. At first, that bothered me, and I discussed this with Cliff, a friend who was an attorney. Cliff was a brilliant guy, caring and with great insight. I trusted his opinions. Cliff's advice was to forget about legal action because probably nothing would have made much of a difference. He recommended that I try to move on.

CHAPTER 9

Dad began to play bridge more and more. It was something he could still do, and he enjoyed the competition and the mental stimulation. Conveniently, there were bridge games in his apartment building, where a lot of older people lived. Sometimes I joined him; he liked that. His body's rigidity, slowness, tremors and instability increased. He somehow still shopped and even drove a little. I was amazed but frightened by the danger.

He refused to admit that he had any limitations. Nothing I could do or say altered his recalcitrant attitude and obdurate behavior. Even when I tried asking him why, for instance, he was not playing golf anymore, just to test him, he would evade the question. His intractable denials were inveterate, and they were hazardous to his well being. I really do not know to this day what his innermost thoughts were about his illness. That is the way my father was.

I tried to spend as much time as I could with him in the latter years, in part because of his condition. Dad could barely get up, start to move or stand on his feet with stability. He grasped for things to pull himself upright. He fell once on a little ice next to the car, when, against my wishes, we went out to dinner. I had dropped him at the restaurant door, but as I was driving away to park the car, I saw in the rear view mirror that he was stumbling. He fell backward onto the concrete sidewalk. Other than a slight amount of blood, there was, amazingly, no real injury from that startling fall.

He eventually consented to take some of the neuro- active medications prescribed by his neurologists, but he was never faithful to the dosages. He was always trying to deny that he had a problem and trying to remain as defiantly independent as he possibly could.

When Dad heard that I was going to a football game at RFK Stadium in Washington with my young son and a few adult friends, he wanted to go, too. This was part of the 1994 soccer World Cup, played in the United States. It was the kind of thing he had always done. He was unwilling to voluntarily forego much of what he enjoyed. Against my better judgment, we took him along. Four grown men wound up carrying him upstairs, to his seat, and out of the stadium later. He simply could not walk on his own.

Dad refused any nursing assistance. I took him to see senior citizen housing with built-in levels of nursing care, but he would not agree' to move from his apartment. This battle went on for years, with the disease clearly taking more of a toll as time went by. Sometimes, when the nursing aides I obtained for him came, he refused to let them in even though he needed the help and was entitled to it. He knew who they were and when they were coming, and he was diabolical in his disdain for the assistance he so desperately needed. He also refused to use the cane and walker that the doctors prescribed and that I had gotten for him. I continually cajoled, cautioned and castigated him about using them.

Mentally, Dad was as sharp as ever. Physically, he was trying to compensate in any meager way he could in order to cling to his independence.

About a year after Mom's death, Dad fortuitously met a lovely lady in his building while playing bridge. For the next five years, they had what I thought was a wonderful relationship. She was about his age but quite healthy except that she could not see well because of macular degeneration. Sight, though, was something my father had little trouble with, and in a way they were a perfect match. I had never seen my father so happy. Phyllis was a very dear person, and she was great for Dad. I think his charm and wit was something of an inspiration to her. She had lost her husband many years earlier. This relationship sustained Dad for those five years or so, while the Parkinson's Disease was eating away at his nervous system. In the end, even Phyllis encouraged my father to consent to a nursing facility where he could live more safely and comfortably. We explored every possible arrangement with him, but he refused to budge.

I received an urgent call one night from someone in my father's apartment building, asking me to come right away. I was there in about twenty minutes, and my father was totally incoherent. Someone had found him lying face down on the floor near the bank of elevators, not far from the mailboxes. I can only speculate that he tripped while trying to walk without assistance, and fell face forward. With his advanced Parkinson's Disease, that explanation seemed entirely likely.

After this emergency department visit, I moved Dad to another hospital in the area where he remained for about four months, quite a long stay in an acute-care facility. Neurologist after neurologist saw him, and he underwent every test known to medical science. In the end, the conclusion was that the fall had damaged his brain in some way that was invisible on X-ray and MRI and by any other means of medical detection. He never had a stroke.

I moved him to a nursing home, where he remained for

about six months. He did not know where he was or, perhaps, even who he was. I believe he recognized my face in some way. Words came out of his mouth, some in response to speech, but none of it was rational. Eventually, he lost his ability to recognize me in any meaningful way. All of this was as stunning as it was tragic. It seemed so sudden.

Dad was moved to another nursing facility and then, yet again, to another -- about as pleasant a place as could have been expected under the circumstances. He languished in his semi-vegetative state for about five more years, quite a long ordeal. The last home was not in the Washington, D.C. area, but near Philadelphia, near my brother. Dad was moved because I could no longer be around to watch over him. His condition was pitiful. The reason for my absence was horrific.

One day, as if somehow he knew his time had come, he stopped eating. By that Friday, he was gone. That day was almost exactly fourteen years from the day of Mom's phone call summoning me to New York City to find out what was wrong.

CHAPTER 10

It was still early in 1993. The economy was good. Pillco, the company that Art and I had formed, had finally arrived. We had won the large LAIS patent infringement lawsuit in federal court. We had also won a case the year before against another manufacturer of our patented technology, Candela Laser. With our patents once again affirmed by a jury verdict and a judge's decree, we dominated the field, which looked set to grow exponentially.

I was, in some ways, on top of the world. I was about fifteen years into a medical practice in the Washington, D.C. area. However, the back stabbing by competitors, which had started in the early 1980s, only intensified.

The pressures of building the practice, running the companies and handling my parents' illnesses had been immense. My father continued to suffer and worsen. I was, by default, his primary care- giver still at this time, another demanding role I had been thrust into.

Even closer to home, another disaster was unfolding that I had been largely ignoring for almost a decade. That turned out in the end to be my undoing. I have longed since rued my failure to be more proactive when it began.

Kim was 12, and she was a bright, cheerful girl. David, three years Kim's junior, was shy and less sure of himself, but beginning to establish his own identity. Three years earlier, I had coaxed him out of his shell by coaching the neighborhood soccer team for six year olds. I knew nothing about soccer, although I had seen it played at high levels in other countries and had enjoyed it. I coached in order to get him to participate, and that worked. David scored the first team goal of the season. That was sheer luck, but it kept him interested.

I had two active, demanding children, both doing well in their private school, but I had a wife whose situation was deteriorating. As time went on, she was able to do less and less, and the horror of what was happening finally became unbearable.

Something had to give. In the end, everything gave, but in the 1980s it had not been as clear to me as it became by the mid-1990s. Tragically, even then it was not as clear to me as it should have been.

Just before Mom died in 1988, I had decided to sell my private medical practice. This was a major step and a departure from my lifelong intentions. It did not mean that I would stop practicing Ophthalmology, but the practice was a burden not only because of the time requirements and the pressure, but also because of the increasing emotional and physical demands of Wendy's situation. I needed to downsize my obligations.

I discussed this with my dying mother, partly to ask her advice but also, in a way, to ask her permission. My mother had lived with us during the mid-1980s, after her cancer recurrence had been diagnosed, and had seen my wife's problems develop. Later, I believed that Mom had been prescient enough to see what was coming, and that it worried her. This was the last thing she needed as she languished with terminal cancer. She suggested I sell the practice, thinking that it could help simplify my life. She imagined that I could go down that road again when circumstances changed. But my mother's deathbed hopes would never come to be.

There was a tsunami on the horizon, and neither Mom nor I could foresee how to escape it.

With some difficulty, I sold the Atlantic Eye Center and the building I had had constructed to house it. I found a part-time position in Ophthalmology in the greater Washington area around 1989, and that lasted for six years. It allowed me to continue in the game while freeing up time for other matters, of which there were plenty.

Suddenly, after the LAIS victory and all that had gone wrong, things seemed wonderful again in 1993. Little did I know that my family was about to become the unwitting victim of a genetic abnormality. I understood little about that problem in those days.

Just after David was born in 1983, my wife began to suffer from a common but insidious illness: major depressive disorder. This condition is not always diagnosed and not often effectively treated. It can be genetic in origin. The brain's neuronal chemical uptake is abnormal. The symptoms may include lethargy, sadness, inability to perform many everyday tasks, difficulty working, feelings of hopelessness, loss of self-esteem, appetite and libido. It sometimes masquerades as other non-psychiatric illnesses. Since mental illness is so stigmatized, it often goes undetected in part because the disease's victims do not seek help. General physicians often do not recognize the condition even when it is brought to them by an affected patient with vaguely defined complaints.

CHAPTER 11

Before I married Wendy, she told me that her father had died of a heart attack when she was a teenager in the Buffalo, New York area. I discovered the truth much, much later. Her father had been put in a mental hospital by his wife, Wendy's mother, and later committed suicide. He was a victim of manic depression. His family had been his victim, and so had part of his community. He had physically abused my ex-wife and others.

Manic depression is one of the less common depressive disorders. The patient has manic phases and depressive phases. In the manic cycle, the patient is often hyper-active, even to the point of self-exhaustion. He or she may be abusive or physically violent but is in severe denial. The patient schemes. This is very different from the "black hole" the severely depressed patient feels he or she is in. The manic depressive, or bipolar patient, hates the depressive part of the illness, the way it feels and debilitates him or her.

In the manic cycle, the person may feel on top of the world and has not got a clue that he or she is dysfunctional and hurtful and destructive; the patient believes that nothing is wrong. This helps explain why these people often fail to take their medicine. Their non- compliance with the medicine only makes things worse, and they remain barely aware of their problem. The manic also may experience extremes in the amount of sleep and/or in appetite for food or sex. Manics may be psychotic, with paranoid delusions, delusions of grandeur or other delusions. Psychotic delusional states are, by definition, detached from reality.

Manic depressives often cycle between the two poles of their illness. Their behavior can be destructive when they are manic; when they are severely depressed, they may harm themselves.

Eventually, it became clear that my wife had crossed the line into manic depression. Later in 1993, she had mostly shed the deeper depression, and the mania began to dominate her behavior. She had earlier, in the late 1980s and early 1990s, gone into remission. But in 1993, she became hypermanic.

I am not a psychiatrist, but I got plenty of hands-on training at home. It was not until later that I realized that I had been co- dependent for years. That is when someone close to the ill person acts in ways more appropriate to the other person's sickness than would be normal. The co-dependent plays a role in the illness and is not helping to combat it. Co- dependency is common. In the late 1980s, I went to a psychologist for help coping with Wendy's depression and emerging mania. I was persuaded to join a support group for spouses. That helped a lot; I realized that I was not the only one whose world had been turned upside down by a mate's manic depression.

Wendy went through a series of psychiatrists over the years, probably a dozen or so I knew about, and who knows how many others? Whenever one told her she needed more treatment, electroshock therapy or hospitalization, she denied it and fired that doctor. It was diabolical. There were many times when I tried to intervene with the psychiatrists she was seeing, but each time, she would rebuff me. Or, some of them would turn me away, invoking patient confidentiality. In such circumstances, who benefits from that secrecy? That lack of communication only helps to enable the mental illness's manifestations and quash what might be useful in combating it. For Wendy, it was part stigma, part denial and part machination, I believe, in retrospect. For years, I did not understand the significance of that pattern. Maybe that was because of my own denial that my life was being threatened by my wife's illness.

I even helped Wendy keep her problem a secret, although that was not necessarily my intention. I helped her perpetuate the deception of her normality. I did this out of respect but also out of ignorance. I, too, did not want my family stigmatized. Even more than that, I was terrified by the prospect that my children might have inherited this genetic curse, which might appear later in their lives, destroying them and their loved ones. To this day, I am haunted by that. The entire family was trapped, and my wife became the unwitting villain in our tragedy.

After Wendy's relative remission around 1989, perhaps fostered by one of the many antidepressive medications she had been taking, I was lulled back to sleep. A five-year-old nightmare seemed to be over, and I thought that she was "cured." It was no more than wishful thinking. And so, by the middle of 1993, life seemed relatively wonderful.

I do not know what drastic steps I could have taken to try to avoid the then future consequences of this horrible illness. I know today that it is highly unlikely that I could have prevented much of what happened. I thought then that I had sacrificed a lot. Looking back, I should have tried even harder to salvage something.

Wendy's clinical condition took a significant turn for the worse that year. Whether in some tangible way things could have been different for Kim and David, I can not know. That haunts me even now.

CHAPTER 12

In late 1993, my wife's chemical-imbalance time bomb finally went off.

Wendy had been suicidal in the 1980s, but she had not succeeded. What would have happened to our family if I had not saved her when she intentionally overdosed back then?

Towards the end of 1993, Wendy turned manic, with severe paranoid delusions. She became verbally abusive and then physically violent. She would hit, kick and shove the children.When I intervened, I became the victim. But I was her favorite target. Our formerly loving marriage and mutual respect fell prey to these episodes, which occurred without provocation or warning. Her behavior was uncontrollable, dangerous, destructive and largely still a secret from the outside world. There were neighbors who heard things. I have no idea what they thought; in any case, they never attempted to intervene.

For nearly two years, I suffered physical attacks. Wendy punched me and threw scalding water at me and almost anything else she could get her hands on.

Two Washington, D.C. area forensic psychiatrists writing reports about my wife's mental health to be submitted to the court as evidence stated:

"Wendy has a major mental illness, a Bipolar I Disorder (Manic- Depressive), an aggressive, impulsive, persecutory delusional, irrational, physical assaultive, self- centeredness, lack of sensitivity to the feelings of another, lack of appropriate behavioral controls with total lack of insight and judgment." She has a"genetic familial history of this condition."

The paranoid delusions were a "psychic manifestation where the patient experiences ideas, feelings and attitudes of her own as though they were in another person and not in herself."

"The persecution is focused on Dr. Fox, her husband, without her capacity to reflect rationally on alternative explanations for circumstances and events."

She was also described as "being totally unaware of her own hostility and provocation" and as "making false accusations of the other person, in order to try to stop him, persecute him and punish him, vilifying and villainizing him, as if to substitute him for her."

Wendy was "likely to cause serious physical harm toward her victims, with extremely violent potential."

My wife kept a large array of psychiatric experts' reports from me while we were married; I discovered some of them later.

There was no treatment to which she would agree. None of her awful behavior was mitigated.

This is not so uncommon. Mental illness destroys people's lives, and those who suffer the most are often the people closest to the ones with the disease. These sick people are dangerous to society, even if their problem is unnoticed for a long period of time. They are ticking time bombs, and the societal cost is surely great in terms of dollars lost due to poor productivity, physical destruction, indirect costs for the families of these individuals and in many other ways. All too often, the health-care system ignores them. This is a gross societal failure, not just in the health care and mental health care systems but also in the justice system, the social service environment and in the workplace.

We tried family counseling. That usually does not work in cases of this type of mental illness. Wendy fired accusations at me and deflected any discussion about her own behavior. She was in complete denial. Those sessions only seemed to make things worse.

As far as I could tell by looking at family insurance claims, Wendy had gone through a slew of psychiatrists. Eventually, she found a "psychopharmacologist." This is a psychiatrist who treats affective conditions such as mania and depressive mood disorders, with drugs only, eschewing talk therapy. The psychopharmacologist measures a treatment's success by the level of the prescribed drug in the patient's bloodstream. Unfortunately, in some cases, this has little correlation with the person's well-being. Wendy would go for brief visits with this therapist, and when he asked how she was doing, she would say "fine." He would order more blood drawn and send her off, writing whatever prescription he thought might be appropriate. Her behavior did not improve.

My wife's mania, severe anger and violence started to become noticeable outside our home. During my last couple of years with Wendy, I heard over and over from other people that she must be "having a bad day." I found out later that when Wendy was questioned about her behavior, she claimed I had made her that way.

Once Wendy told several people that she was late because I had forgotten to pick up her new dress from the department store where she bought it and had it altered. Not only did I not know about the new dress, but I had been out of town the whole time on business. There were often circumstances where Wendy simply blamed me, no matter what had really happened.

Wendy worked as a speech therapist in a public school. In the 1980s, she also had had a very successful private practice. She had to give that up when she was overwhelmed by depression. At the time, everyone thought Wendy wanted to spend more time at home with the kids and did not need to work, anyway. People had no idea that her relationship with the two children had become increasingly abusive or that she was mentally ill.

The kids had become co-dependent in their own way. Kim perceived that her mother was in psychological trouble, although children can not understand bipolar disorder. It is hard enough for adults to understand. But Kim's reaction was protective of her mother, experts later explained to me. Kim sensed that Wendy could not withstand criticism or handle blame for her circumstances. She simply could not take any responsibility. Kim understood that it was easier for me to bear being a victim and that that was the way things were.

David tried not to take sides. He tried to ignore the situation as much as he could. That proved to be impossible.

How the children understood their abuse by Wendy, I can not know. To my knowledge, they never had therapy of any kind. That should have been ordered by the court.

Children who live with manic depressives need counseling and guidance but often they do not get it. Bipolar parents can not understand their children's needs; that would require the sick parents to admit their own problem, something they deny. The non-bipolar parent often does not have the control to make certain that the children get the therapy they need.

Wendy rejected any real counseling; the family therapy we did turned out to be an opportunity for her to rant and rave about me, then leave the session even angrier than she was in the beginning.

Wendy opposed any outside influence on the children because she instinctively knew that outsiders would see her sick behavior. She put up a wall of denial and delusion to protect herself from reality.

There were times at work when Wendy "flew off the handle," and she was warned that she might be fired from the school. She sought help at least once that I found out about -- from a family friend. He was a well-known labor attorney who helped her talk her way out of that jam at the school board. Her whole life had turned into a relentless effort to cover up her illness.

Wendy's family was part of the problem. Her mother never came to grips with the abuse she had endured at the hands of Wendy's manic-depressive father years earlier in the Buffalo area. He had also physically abused Wendy. Wendy never talked about that, not even with psychiatrists, as far as I knew. Her mother, Doris, could not stand the thought that family history was repeating itself, and she feared that her daughter would wind up in a mental institution or commit suicide. That is precisely what Doris told me.

She preferred sticking her head in the sand to pushing for treatment. It was easier for Doris to blame someone else than to confront the ugly reality. Bipolar disorder is hereditary.

Wendy's only other sibling, her sister Sharon, suffered from severe depression and very possibly full blown bipolar disease, as well. Sharon provided no helpful insight into her sister's situation.

I had no clue as to how to deal with this situation with people outside the family unit.

I went into counseling in order to try to handle this nightmare. I did not feel comfortable discussing it with close friends. I tried a few times, but they either did not want to hear about it or could not believe that it was true. Even friends who were doctors denied that this could be happening. Even later, when I discussed with them some aspects from her medical records, they could not believe it.

By 1994, I began to document some of the physical abuse I suffered at Wendy's hands. I was strongly advised by some professionals to call the police when she attacked me, although I found this repugnant. I never saw the police as a solution. Eventually, I began to hope that at least she might get a "wakeup call," if I brought in the police. Nothing could have been further from the truth.

By autumn 1995, I had filed thirty- four police reports with the Arlington, Virginia County law enforcement department, all documenting her physical abuse of me. That was less than a year after I had started contacting the police when she assaulted me at home almost weekly. I never asked to have her arrested because I could not bear the thought. It seemed ludicrous to me for the police to "solve" this kind of problem.

Later, I realized that I had been inappropriately protective of Wendy. This turned out to be a big mistake. Most people could not believe that there was such a violent woman in their midst. But, a female police officer who took one of my assault reports, told me that one of her male colleagues also had a manic-depressive, physically abusive wife. Most police officers, like most other people, found it hard to believe that a man could be the victim and a woman the aggressor in domestic violence. Our situation was the opposite of the stereotype.

By 1994 I was thinking of leaving my wife and ending the marriage. I would have left sooner if not for the kids. For a long time, I thought the family had to be preserved no matter what. And that any other outcome would mean that I had failed. My own parents had been unhappily married, but they had stayed together until the end.

The damage to my own little family had already been done -- by one small genetic mutation.

The physical abuse continued, and there was no solution on the horizon. I talked Wendy into going into mediation with an old friend of ours, who was a mediator and an accountant. He tried very hard to reach some sort of harmonious reconciliation. However, it was clear from the beginning that Wendy could not come to terms with reality. She had to blame me for everything she believed was wrong. She persisted in attempting to extract impossible and often delusional concessions from me to satisfy her sick psyche, such as insisting I pay her $10 million in cash if we separated. She could not and has not ever taken responsibility for her behavior. She insisted throughout that I take blame for events that never even happened and that I admit to having beliefs I never held. There had to be an end to this vicious cycle. It came suddenly in late 1995.

CHAPTER 13

In the late 1980s when Art and I set up Pillco to hold and license our patents, our lawyers told us to make the business a limited partnership, which we did. I was one of the limited partners.

Art decided that instead of being a limited partner himself, he would create an entity that would enable his family to be a limited partner in Pillco. That entity was called the Coster Family Limited Partnership or CFLP. The CFLP had two general partners, Art and his wife, Virginia, and three limited partners, their adult children: Jeff, Mark and Michelle.

Only general partners can manage limited partnerships. The limited partners, something like shareholders in a corporation, do not have that power.

There was a separate entity that functioned as Pillco's general partner, and I operated it.

Art and I had known each other for more than ten years by the late 1980s, and we occasionally socialized. I also knew Art's family.

Wendy and I were invited to Michelle's wedding and reception at a large hotel in downtown Washington, D.C. in the winter of 1995. During the reception, Michelle thanked us for attending and for " helping to make our family wealthy with Pillco." This was a lovely gesture by the bride, and I had not expected it.

Ominously, Wendy was "acting up" at the reception, cursing me and hurling accusations at me throughout the evening.

We were supposed to spend that night at the hotel, even though we lived across the Potomac River in Arlington, Virginia, only a quarter hour drive from there. We returned to our hotel room at about two thirty in the morning, as the festivities were dying down. Wendy was ranting and raving, and I could not go to sleep. At about four in the morning she announced that we should just go home. So I got dressed, and we left.

At about 4:15 a.m., I was driving west on Rock Creek Parkway towards the Chain Bridge that crosses into Virginia. Rock Creek Parkway twists and turns through a small forest adjacent to the picturesque Potomac. The road was a little icy and not very well lit. Wendy was fiddling with something in her handbag.

I turned the car toward the right, casting my eyes in that direction and saw something shiny coming from the passenger seat where Wendy was sitting. The object was coming straight towards my chest. With my left hand still on the steering wheel, my right hand reached for what turned out to be Wendy's hand, grasping a steak knife aimed at my heart.

We skidded off the road, into a shallow ditch on the right. I was still clutching Wendy's wrist. Then she dropped the knife, and I grabbed it. My wife was trying to kill me!

As I write this twenty-five years later, I am still shocked, maybe even more today than then, when I moved quickly and instinctively.

It took me a long, long time to take that in. It took even longer yet to piece this together with the previous violence, the delusions and the psychotic behavior. Only ten years earlier, this woman had been a loving wife and mother. Even then, I did not fully understand her terrible illness.

Why was this my fate, my wife's fate, that of our family? I still do not know, except that it was bad luck. The "clinical" part of the story, I came to understand better.

I suffered emotionally from that attack and still do. I have a kind of post-traumatic stress syndrome (PTSD). I am not particularly afraid of kitchen knives or of women, nor do I suffer general physical symptomatology. But I have had trouble concentrating on certain things ever since.

In the early 1990s, I had trouble sleeping because I feared Wendy would attack me in my sleep; she did once. But worst of all, the greatest pain and that which is most difficult for me to handle, concerns my children and what happened to them. I was an adult when this came to pass, while they were children who did not understand what was happening. They will not ever be able to come to grips with it even though they are grown up now.

The marriage, to someone who turned into the devil, ended. I found other, better partners.

If Wendy had succeeded in killing me, she would probably still be in jail in the District of Columbia. As it turned out twenty- five years later, I was consigned to suffer and she was still free.

CHAPTER 14

After the shock of my wife's attempt to stab me, I was not able to think entirely clearly for the next two or three years. I realized that only later.

After that fateful event, I did things I had not only never planned, but also never even imagined I might do. I was in a kind of free fall. I tried to figure out what had happened and what might happen next, and I groped for ways to deal with it.

I kept the knife from the attack.

After Wendy tried to kill me, we went home. It never occurred to me to drive to the nearest police station; I am not sure why not. From then on, I was more afraid than ever to be around her, and very fearful for the children.

I found a divorce lawyer. This turned out to be a fiasco.

Philip was nearing the end of a long family law career in the Arlington, Virginia area. A couple of people had mentioned him to me. Sometimes if you last long enough in your field, you get to be well known regardless of the quality of your work. Sometimes surviving equates with victory. Philip was jovial, a mood that did not quite fit my own in those days. He liked telling stories about his former sexual escapades with women, some of whom had been or still were judges on the local bench where we were going to be litigating the divorce. He had been married about four times. Sometimes divorce lawyers practice what they preach.

We filed for divorce in Arlington, Virginia. This turned out to be horrendous legal advice that only made my already greatly disrupted life much worse. There were four judges on that bench, and we wound up with Benjamin Kendrick who, it turned out, rivaled my wife in wreaking havoc and destruction.

Philip and I went to the U.S. Attorney's Office in the District of Columbia, where I swore out a criminal complaint against Wendy for what the District Attorney called "premeditated attempted murder," a felony. Wendy was arrested in Washington, D.C. for that crime, but only a year and a half later, in 1997. Since she lived in Virginia, all of ten minutes away, the authorities apparently could not be bothered to apprehend her there, even for attempted murder. Such is the speed of justice, and the events of my life seemed to prove the adage that justice delayed is justice denied.

We also went to the Arlington County police station where I had previously filed those dozens of complaints about Wendy's attacks on me but had failed to press charges. I had never filed a police complaint against her for violence against the children since I only heard about most of that from them and did not witness much of it. Much later, I heard other anecdotal tales about that type of violence by Wendy from others. But now that my prior complaints were no longer fresh, the police were reluctant to prosecute her. And Kendrick quickly made sure they did not do that.

He immediately separated the two of us, but he let her stay in our home, with the children! I put most of my things in storage and slept on the sofa in my father's apartment until I found a place to rent. I moved three or four times within that next year.

Many of our friends refused to believe that Wendy could

have done the things she did. In the end, they either took it out on me for bringing them a story such as this, or shunned both of us, as if years of friendship meant nothing under these unusual and embarrassing circumstances. I was deflated, shocked, angry, and left with far fewer friends than I thought I had had.

We choose our friends, as opposed to our relatives and usually our neighbors. For this reason, I thought that friends would be more likely to stand by me. I learned that friendship was not always what I thought and that only a subset of my friends were true. It takes this sort of adversity to come to know which ones fall into which category.

Some of them understood what had happened to my family, and they were there for me. I had both male and female friends who were sympathetic to my suffering and that of the children. I am forever indebted to all of them.

My employees, all of whom were women, were in the supportive group, but maybe paying them a salary buys that kind of thing-- I would like to think not. They also knew me very well. Some of my friends' wives supported me and my side, as if there can be a "side" in severe mental illness. But, obligatorily so, I also began then to make new friends.

My father was too out of it to really understand or help. He and Phyllis were sympathetic, and they gathered that my situation was dire, but that is as far as they could take it at that time in their lives. If this had come earlier on in my father's lifetime, I suspect he would have risen more to the occasion. I thought a lot then, and before and since, too, about my late mother because had she been alive at this time, she would have helped me more. I did not have much other family. No one lived anywhere nearby. Bob was understanding at some levels and has never challenged me in any way about this. But he has his own life, his own family and his own commitments.

I was suddenly very alone.

CHAPTER 15

Wendy's family lived in the Buffalo, New York area in the early 1960s. Her father, Irving Richter, was at the height of his mania wreaking havoc with a lot of people. He was an account-ant who played fast and loose with other people's finances as well as his own family's. He was also violent. I knew nothing about this until after Wendy and I were divorced; her father had died before I met her.

When Irving ran into trouble by helping himself to cli-ents' money, Wendy's mother, Doris, turned to an attorney named William Carnahan for help. He later moved to Wash-ington, D.C., where a desperate Doris sought him out again in 1995. Carnahan knew about the family secret -- the hereditary bipolar disorder -- and learned that the daughter, my wife, had fallen prey to it. Surely, he realized that she had also become violent and had turned her life into a mess. Her marriage was ending, and his help was desperately needed.

When Carnahan learned that I had filed for divorce in Arlington, he connected with a lawyer there named Denman Rucker, who was close to the judge presiding over the case, Benjamin Kendrick. In the 1970s, Rucker was tried and convicted for selling lysergide (LSD) in northern Virginia. Kendrick, then a lawyer, represented Rucker at his trial in Fairfax County, Virginia, next to Arlington County. Kendrick and Rucker had been childhood friends. Kendrick's mother was one of the first female attorneys in Virginia, and Rucker's father had been the County Attorney for Arlington.

According to rumors in legal circles, both Rucker and Kendrick were dealing drugs, but Rucker took the rap for the two of them. Rucker served time in the Virginia penitentiary. When he left prison, he got his law license back, thanks to his father's influence, according to rumor. Kendrick therefore owed Rucker big time.

Carnahan arranged for Rucker to represent Wendy, and Rucker arranged for Kendrick to hear the divorce case. That type of judge- shopping is not supposed to happen, but everyone knows that it does.

Ethically, Kendrick had no business judging the divorce case based on his prior attorney- client relationship with Rucker, to say nothing of the rest of their relationship. Rucker did not normally do divorce cases. His practice consisted of getting court referrals, often from Kendrick, for small cases or motions where a local lawyer was needed to represent someone. Rucker was not exactly the most distinguished member of the Virginia Bar.

But then, Kendrick was not a distinguished judge. "Kendrick is the most reversed judge in the history of the Commonwealth of Virginia," one of my early divorce lawyers told me. His decisions were overturned by Virginia Appeals Courts more often than any other circuit court judge's in the more than 200-year history of the state. He had been on the bench a little over ten years, while some others, who had far fewer decisions overturned, served for as much as nearly sixty years.

It is not uncommon for some judges to serve well into their twilight years. Some of them continue to work even though they have become senile; some have been known to fall asleep during a trial. I had seen that with Judge Winston on the Arlington bench in the 1980s in my case against Arlington Hospital.

Kendrick was not old and senile at the time of the divorce. He distinguished himself by his unfettered arrogance, rancor, disdain, hatefulness, mendacity, malevolence and spite. Court transcripts and descriptions by lawyers before him give vivid evidence of this. That he was appointed and re- appointed to the bench by Virginia legislators is an embarrassment.

Kendrick and his buddy Rucker ensured that my children remained in the custody of a violently mentally ill person. Kendrick refused to admit into the court proceedings psychiatric testimony or any other evidence of Wendy's illness. He blocked the criminal justice system there from acting as it should have against her.

For the next ten years of his career as a judge, Kendrick, at Rucker's behest, on behalf of his client, did all he could to destroy my life. He made a mockery of the judicial system in the process.

A scholarly legal analysis of Kendrick's handling of my divorce and business excoriated the judge. Quoting that memorandum from other court records:

Kendrick "demonstrated the utter lack of fundamental fairness" to Dr. Fox and others, wrote Marc Zell, a distinguished international lawyer.

"The judge ignored the legal requirement for the court to have jurisdiction over parties, savagely pursued counsel with contempt citations and the prospect of fines and imprisonment for doing

nothing more than interposing a jurisdictional challenge or assert-
ing a judicial appeal, intimidated both parties and their attorneys,
was hell- bent on ignoring the most fundamental rules of fair play
and substantial justice in ramrodding through decrees that went
far beyond the jurisdiction of his court, severely abused the rights
of Dr. Fox and others, posited time and again false facts and deci-
sions utterly unsupported by the law, taxed the limits of credulity,
gutted the jurisdictional foundations of the litigation before him,
published order after order totally void as a matter of Virginia law,
repeatedly openly stating on the record that his ultimate desire is to
'put Dr. Fox behind bars for as long as possible,' and then den(ied
Dr. Fox) his day in court unless and until that [the jailing of Dr. Fox]
(were to) happen, and, in the end, conducted proceedings after pro-
ceedings little better than a kangaroo court," Zell wrote in those later
court proceedings.

Why did I get this treatment from Kendrick? He was
bought for the occasion by Wendy Richter Fox, who had no
business bringing up children, deserved to go to prison and
should have been under significant psychiatric supervision.

It is unknown whether any of the treatments suggested
to her time and again by psychiatrists would have made any
difference in her condition.

She might have remained a financial burden for me even if
there had been a fair judge deciding the divorce, but all of this
would have paled in comparison to what happened, thanks to
the intervention of Kendrick, a corrupt judge of the worst kind
imaginable.

Wendy's illness demanded that someone other than herself be blamed for all that had happened. I was the obvious victim. Kendrick became Wendy's accomplice. One can not cover
up severe mental illness by applying severe wayward justice.
The former Wendy Fox is still psychotic and the former judge
Kendrick is still the biggest disgrace in Virginia judicial history.

CHAPTER 16

It turned out that the Richter scandal in Buffalo was not the only family secret that had been scrupulously kept from me by Wendy and her mother.

Doris Richter, widowed after Irving's suicide, was searching for a way out of Buffalo and the family's disgrace. She was introduced to a man in Ohio who had recently lost his wife to cancer and was growing lonely in a small town. He owned some department stores and was quite wealthy. Doris set her sights on this guy. They met, one thing led to another, and they married shortly before Wendy and I did in 1975. Doris got out of western New York that way.

There was one obstacle for her, however. That was Karen,

the adopted daughter of her new husband. Karen was fourteen, and she was doing drugs. She had lost her mother to cancer not too many years before her father's remarriage to Doris. Having this new woman on the scene did not help Karen, either. Doris could not handle Karen, nor could she handle the competition. She realized quickly that if Karen could somehow be dispensed with, her pathway to a small fortune would become much easier.

Doris gave Bernie, the husband, an ultimatum: "Either Karen goes or I do." Wendy and I were horrified, and she stopped speaking to her mother for a while after that. Before her illness, Wendy was special. Doris was not. Nonetheless, Doris won, Karen ran away and was never heard from again.

Doris built on that. Bernie established trusts for Doris and her two daughters. At the time I filed for divorce, Wendy had other homes on both coasts, at least one in the Washington, D.C. area and another in fashionable Coronado, California -- if not others I still do not know about -- and a big fat trust fund, besides.

Unbeknownst to me while we were married, Wendy had several million dollars. I had paid all of our costs -- for the family, my attorneys, sometimes hers, her psychiatrists, moving, professional expenses and more while she had a secret fortune and other homes. She also got all that Kendrick could rip off from me or anyone else he or she could victimize.

My savings were dwindling, my children refused to see me, Kendrick was trying to make sure I could not be with them and Wendy was trying to deprive me of everything, including my life.

Emotionally, I was on a knife's edge. My Ophthalmology situation dried up, probably coincidentally. My associate and his wife, both friends, never showed any ill will towards me. They were reorganizing the practice, bringing in someone new, a young guy just out of training, and there was no longer any need for my services there.

Pillco's name was changed to Interlase LP by our attorneys. We had problems with Spectranetics, then our main licensee- manufacturer. But there were other companies to license, and we were still engaged in promising research. I hoped to continue that, somewhere, somehow.

I had always supported my children in as grand a style as I could manage, as everyone who knew us could see. They went to fine private schools and, financially, lacked for nothing.

Suddenly, my income was much more limited, and I had huge expenses, mostly for lawyers, as well as the possibility of supporting a severely mentally ill, soon-to-be ex- wife who might never get better. I did not know then about her millions, and if Kendrick knew about all her money, he ignored it.

The first thing Kendrick did was to order me to pay more than $10,000 a month in child support, an amount equal to more than five times the Virginia norm in our financial situation. This was purely punitive and explicitly illegal.

I considered practicing Ophthalmology elsewhere in the United States. However, Philip and several other lawyers warned me that Kendrick would try to throw me in jail if I did not come up with the child support. This might not have been such a grave threat a couple of years earlier, if I had moved to another state. But in 1994, Bill and Hillary Clinton succeeded in making child-support violations a federal crime, with no defense possible. I was advised by one of my lawyers that for "my offense," for not being able to pay more than $10,000 a month in grossly illegal child support, conveniently and diabolically labeled as such by Kendrick specifically for my maximum detriment, I would have to serve three and a third years in a federal prison. This was besides the Writ of Ne Exeat, prohibiting the target from leaving the State of Virginia and contempt citations from Kendrick, all of which were soon to come.

Given this new legal landscape, Kendrick could turn me into a criminal without any recourse by setting the amount of child support beyond my means. He knew I had no right of appeal until the divorce case was over; he later ensured that even afterwards, I probably would not be able to appeal, either.

I consulted again with Cliff, who was very close to this situation as my friend and one of my lawyers. He told me to leave the country, to go as far as possible, and try to forget all this and start over. He, too, was afraid of what might happen to me if I stayed in Virginia or anywhere else in the United States. Some friends agreed that I should leave while others said I should stay to fight in the courts for what was right. I was warned by other attorneys, some of them well acquainted with Kendrick, that I probably could not afford to stay and fight and that, in any case, I would never win in those Virginia courts.

I was probably not able to make the best decisions in the midst of all that turmoil. But I had to do something, and fast. Philip, too, told me I was in jeopardy anywhere in the United States, and he also suggested that I leave the country -- strange advice, perhaps, to hear from your own divorce lawyer. If I had not left, I might still be in Arlington County jail. Kendrick had imprisoned others for no reason, sometimes for very lengthy periods, and lawyers could not assure me that they would be able to get me out, given the legal environment.

Many months after the knife attack, I bought a one-way plane ticket to Nassau, Bahamas. I was 49 years old. I imagined I would be there for a few months and have some breathing room while I waited to see what happened. I wanted to be reunited with my children, but I knew I would have to win the divorce, and that was not likely. I thought that perhaps I could win on appeal. I hoped that it would not take much time and that I could wait it out in Nassau, where I would be safe, less than thirty- three miles from the United States' shore but legally in another world.

Because non-payment of child support was not a crime in the Bahamas, I could not be extradited. In most countries, it was not a crime; it was a civil matter. And I simply could not come close to paying that amount.

I had to remind myself that my wife was the attempted murderer, not me; I was only the designated child support scofflaw.

I never imagined that I would never return to the United States or that I would never see my children again. At least, I did not want to believe that that was going to be my fate.

CHAPTER 17

"Dear David,

It may be hard to understand, but I am excited about being able to write to you now that you are at college and my letter won't be intercepted. David, I'm going to start with just some simple words, and I hope we can continue from there. You can believe what I write or not, be moved or not, and agree or disagree. Although it may have been made very easy for you to forget, I am your father, and I love you very much.

So much has happened since we were last together more than six years ago. This has not been a normal situation, but, tragically, it is the one that happened to us. You don't know me after all of this time, you can not. But I want you to get to know me, and, I want to learn much more about you.

David, please take a first step and send me a reply, anything at all. You can't imagine how important it is for me. Remember, I am not angry. I love you. The time is here, and the time is right. Stick one toe in the water, and take that first step. This next part is up to you, but you can do it, David, and I am here to help where necessary.

Love,

Dad"

That was an email I sent to my son when he was in college in the early 2000s. I agonized over what to write and consulted a psychologist about it. David had been in his mother's custody since 1995 when our tragic marriage abruptly ended. Wendy had prevented the children from having any contact with me. Not only was that the way she wanted it, the court empowered her to do it.

I got a reply to my email, telling me he was at the University of Wisconsin, mentioning a couple of classes he was taking and that he was enjoying being there. He did not say much else. The emails went back and forth for a few weeks. In his last email, David informed me that he "just couldn't do this" and told me I would "never hear from or see him again." Since then, nearly twenty years have passed without any communication.

With Kim, it was worse. She was not inclined even to briefly re-connect. The two of them had become severely "parentally alienated."

Columbia University School of Medicine psychiatrist Richard Gardner wrote the definitive book about Parental Alienation Syndrome, in which an emotionally abusive, mentally ill parent manipulates the children to turn them against the other parent. Once the sick parent's lies are instilled in the children, their alienation from the other parent may be lifelong. The children may also suffer from other psychological problems as a result of Parental Alienation Syndrome.

Gardner called in his book for divorce courts to ensure that a mentally ill, alienating parent does not receive custody of children. An alienating parent's visits with the children should be under strictly controlled circumstances, Dr. Gardner wrote.

That was the only way to prevent Parental Alienation Syndrome, Gardner said. If allowed to develop, PAS becomes permanent. The child is forever damaged by the forced removal of an often loving parent from his or her life.

When Professor Gardner wrote his treatise on Parental Alienation Syndrome in the 1980s, judges, social workers and others involved in child custody cases knew little about this problem.

Gardner defined PAS as "a preoccupation with unreasonable denigration of an alienated parent by children who are alienated by the alienating, other parent." "This," Gardner says, "occurs only in situations where the denigration is not otherwise warranted."

Gardner says that PAS is common, although its severest forms are rarer. Kim and David suffered severe cases, Gardner told me in 1996. He was incredibly negative in his prognosis, saying there was virtually no chance I would ever see my children again given the circumstances I had described to him. In our last session, Gardner said: "Dr. Fox, they are never coming back." He turned out to be right. The loss of my children is the greatest tragedy of my life.

After the almost unspeakable tragedy of October 1995, the attempted murder, I never saw my children. Wendy was given total control, including over my access to the children, and they stopped wanting to see me; she made absolutely certain.

Many people tried to intermediate: psychologists, psychiatrists, professional mediators, lawyers, social workers, teachers, principals, co- workers, friends and, later, we even tried with my children's spouses.

In the beginning, I tried appearing where I thought I might find David and Kim. I tried every way to contact them. I once hired a taxi driver to deliver birthday gifts to my son, when he was still living with his mentally deranged mother. When she saw the driver that evening, she imagined that he came to kidnap David and called the police. The poor guy spent a few hours in jail until saner minds could prevail. I once tried visiting David at school soccer practice. Wendy had him "guarded" by one of her attorneys whose own son was my son's classmate, just in case I might show up. Those were the days before cell phones, and I could not call the house because she controlled the telephone. My letters could not get through, either.

Severe Parental Alienation Syndrome is almost worse than losing a child who dies. That is over; this never ends. The fortune I lost, the wife who was transformed into a monster by mental illness and the friendships that ended after that fateful day in October 1995-- all of that pales compared to what happened to those two children.

The loss of their relationship with a loving father is one thing they can never replace. According to experts I consulted, that loss causes them to try to compensate in other ways that might adversely influence their relationships with others. At the time this was evolving, I had no idea what further consequences, for them, might come out of this.

Counseling has helped me. So have support groups. But the anguish inside me never entirely goes away.

Many people have no relationship with their children. Life goes on. I suspect that the alienated child, even as an adult, suffers more in some ways than does the alienated parent, but I can not prove that, and it probably depends. Many children grow up without parents, or without one parent. My kids, after a time, grew up with only one parent, and that was the one that they should not have had.

Could I have prevented this alienation? The clinical situation suggests that I probably could not have done anything. I hate not having had even the slimmest of chances.

CHAPTER 18

I had worked in England and in Australia, and taught or demonstrated eye surgery in dozens of nations. I had visited more than one hundred countries. The Bahamas was different from anything I had known before.

Nassau had gated communities with homes costing tens of millions of dollars, facing the sea. This is one of those places where the wealthy go to hide or to hide their money. The Bahamas has no taxes. But there is significant poverty there.

The Bahamas expat community might have numbered 70,000, mostly Europeans and Canadians. Most of them were connected to the financial industry in the Bahamas, which has the most banks in the world, attracting wealth from around the globe. After tourism, which includes the cruise industry, banking is by far the Bahamas' biggest business. The country does not have much else.

I tried to adjust to my new world in Nassau. I did not fit in with the very rich or with the very poor. Eventually, I made friends with some pretty well off people, but in the beginning I was lost.

Walking around Nassau the first day, I encountered a local guy selling vacation condos. I stopped, what else did I have to do? He told me about his properties, not that I was interested; mostly, we just talked. When I was about to leave, he said: "My name is Arnold. I realize you are totally new here in the Bahamas, and alone. But I want you to know that Arnold is your friend." As I walked away, I was overwhelmed with emotion -- I was alone in a strange place, and Arnold was my only friend!

I found a furnished apartment. When I went to the Bahamas, I had not considered what an expensive place it was. There were higher cost countries, but not many. The living expenses were eating up my dwindling resources, which were also being drained by attorneys' fees. And my legal problems had just begun.

I got a medical license in the Bahamas, which is very difficult for a foreigner. Local professionals control medical licenses, and they do not want more competition. There were two Ophthalmology practices in Nassau, and I went to meet each doctor. I liked them, and it seemed mutual; they needed part- time help, in retina. I offered something for their practices that they did not have and could not find, locally.

I worked a few mornings a week for the two doctors with their private patients, and they gave me reasonable compensation. The work, and my stay in the Bahamas, turned out to be a lot longer than the few months I originally envisioned.

I also volunteered, running a bare bones Ophthalmology clinic for the indigent once a week at the public hospital.

I continued to run Interlase, talking by phone with Art nearly every day for several years while I remained in Nassau.

We licensed a couple more companies. It was difficult to do research while we were separated, and the necessary facilities did not exist in the Bahamas. We continued to look into some new laser projects we had started experimenting with in Washington, but we were thwarted by these circumstances. I yearned to get that going again as soon as possible, seeing it as an exciting opportunity.

I had met a lovely woman in Washington just before I left the United States. She also imagined that I would come back one day and that something would eventually happen with us. She visited Nassau at least once a month, changing planes in Miami. That arrangement lasted as long as I remained in Nassau, which turned out to be almost five years. Having a companion, especially one from the area where I had lived for over twenty years, helped so much in those days.

My thoughts and a lot of my time were dominated by what was going on in the Washington area -- the divorce case and its aftermath. Kendrick had no intention of conducting anything resembling a divorce case with two sides, despite the heavy issues of mental illness and two minor children. He wanted to punish me on behalf of my wife and her handlers. Wendy said over and over she wanted me in jail or dead. She was acting out her delusion and paying her lawyers to help her carry it out. Her attorneys were perfectly willing to oblige.

For Wendy, there was only one side: hers. She believed that she was the victim of a husband from hell. She never could explain what I had allegedly done, but that did not really matter. For her, I was the devil incarnate. Under Kendrickian justice, no more was required. She soon realized, as did her mother, that she called the shots in Arlington and got whatever she wanted, preferably with my head served up on a silver platter.

There was that out-of-this-world child support. Her side concocted stories about phony companies and attributed them to me. They knew about the real companies, but those were not that interesting to them. They told the court that I had tens of millions of dollars somewhere and that she wanted it. They might have had no small amount of difficulty explaining how I could have earned and saved anywhere near that much. But with Kendrick in charge they did not need to have any proof, nor was there any to be had.

I had always had my family foremost in my plans. I first began to make money in my practice in the 1970s, and when my first child was born in 1980, I established a trust for her that would be expanded to include any subsequent children who might come along. By the time of the divorce, the trust fund had grown to nearly $500,000, and it was invested to keep earning. The trust was a part owner of Intherea, my clinical pharmaceutical testing company, and of Ophthalmology Associates, my legal expert consultancy. The kids would have enough money for as much education as they wanted at the most expensive universities to which they could gain entry.

I also intended that they would have seed money for whatever they did after finishing their university studies, whether it was starting a small business, buying a house or something else. That would ensure that they would have no debt.

I came up with this plan when my daughter was born. The $500,000 would probably have come to be worth well over a million dollars by the time they needed it, because it had been earning quite a bit annually.

What did Kendrick do, almost immediately? He ordered that that trust be turned over to Wendy. That was like opening dozens of bottles of the finest aged wine and mixing it with gasoline. I wanted to fight this, but my lawyer, Philip, said I had better do what the judge ordered and that I could appeal it later. That advice was total crap. There was no hearing, no evidence, no nothing. And in fact there would be no "later." I agonized over this. This was not about me, it was about my children. Kendrick was throwing out their real support and potentially depriving them of their education and more.

Sometimes you make the wrong decision at a crucial time. I signed over the kids' trust money to the court. The next day Kendrick gave it to Wendy. It immediately disappeared into her substantial stash of cash, which I did not then know existed. Not only had my own fate been thrown to the winds, so had that of my children.

I thought I had provided for the kids with the $500,000. I was also paying for the mortgage and household expenses in Arlington, although I could not use the house or be in the same country with my children, who lived there under a reign of terror. I could not afford to pay another more than $10,000 per month in "child support," which was unnecessary in view of the trust money that Kendrick conveniently did not count.

Although I provided money to pay the mortgage, my ex-wife stopped paying it. She then orchestrated a public campaign, weeping openly about how I had caused her to "lose her home" and how she and the kids would be thrown out onto the street. The bank foreclosed, just as she had planned in her delusional scenario.

Wendy hired a mover and moved all of the family stuff, including what remained of my things, to her other home in northern Virginia. I found out that that house had been bought for her with a pile of cash from her mother's husband. I was shocked and hired an investigator to dig deeper. Obviously, Wendy had also furnished her Coronado, California home, too.

Kendrick soon barred me from participating in the divorce case at all. He decided I should produce documents for fake companies "identified" to the court by my wife's lawyers, and, if I did not, I would be held in contempt. What bothered him and my wife was that I left the country before the divorce proceedings even started in earnest.

The absurd illegal child support and other indignities had

already occurred in preliminary hearings, and the handwriting was clearly on the wall.

I did not want to go to jail, and they could not get me in the Bahamas. That was paramount at that time.

So, Kendrick held me in contempt, again and again. This was illegal because I was never served with the obligatory "Rule to show cause," the legally required pre- contempt notice. He also issued a writ of Ne exeat against me. Ne exeat, outlawed in Virginia jurisprudence in the 1870s, literally means "no exit." He ordered me to pay $1 million to leave Virginia, although I had already left.

The purpose of the law had been to prevent a debtor from leaving without paying. Not only was the writ itself illegal, but I had not been in Virginia for more than a year when Kendrick issued it. I had not even been in the United States during that interval. It was just another instance of Kendrick making up facts and making up the law, and going with them.

After that, Kendrick imposed what he called a non- participation sanction against me and my attorneys. That meant we could not participate in the divorce proceedings, only Wendy and her lawyers could. We could not produce evidence, put on witnesses, cross- examine witnesses, make motions, object, nothing. He threatened my lawyers with contempt if they violated the sanction, and they were cowed by his bullying. The court record reflects that out of the blue, from the bench, Kendrick would interrupt whoever was speaking, again and again, and ask "Where's Dr. Fox? Why isn't he in my jail?"

He also made such comments in subsequent cases that should not have been about me. Those were business cases where Kendrick again made certain that I could not participate.

No one who saw any of this, who was not part of Kendrick's crusade, felt that justice was being served. His approach was to bastardize the facts and ignore or make up laws. He prevented parties and their attorneys from participating and intimidated and/or jailed anyone who did not roll over. There was no way to get my case away from this judge, even though his appearance in my divorce matter was improper from the very beginning.

Kendrick practiced his own brand of justice in Virginia. In a later case, he deprived one side of its attorneys, ordered those lawyers to disgorge, or give up, their fees and threatened to throw them in jail for contempt.

He threw some of his victims in jail, fined them until they had nothing left, refused to brook dissent, rejected evidence from one side and issued judgments about people and businesses that were not before his court or were not parties to cases there. Sometimes he issued judgments concerning entities that did not exist. He also issued injunctions, barring parties from suing or otherwise acting on their own behalf.

In the divorce case -- who ever heard of a one- sided divorce trial? -- no facts were submitted by Wendy, Rucker and her team, which included three or four law firms she hired. The facts were deemed unnecessary. There were no witnesses, and my side was barred from participating. The divorce decree was written by Rucker. He presented it to Kendrick at the trial, and the judge signed it without even reading it, as indicated by the court records. That farce occurred in April 1997.

Kendrick also ordered me to give Wendy millions of dollars that she alleged amounted to half of our marital assets, but we never had that much money. Again, no facts were presented to prove the amount of the marital assets. I was saddled with an impossible burden at a time when I found myself essentially out of work and with little in the way of professional opportunities, no home, displaced, hardly any possessions, no family and barely any friends.

If Kendrick's cause had been just and only his means had been crude, there might have been some reason for what he did. But this was a hit job, ordered by a wealthy psychotic and carried out by a sadistic judge masquerading as a public servant.

Meanwhile, Wendy had the kids. I heard from neighbors and families of other children, she was behaving violently toward Kim and David, thoroughly unfettered and unmonitored. She did not get the more than $10,000 a month in child support that I could not pay, but she had her two homes in Virginia and California, her outsized trust fund from her mother's husband and a new beau, who also had a big home in Washington, D.C., not to mention regular money for the mortgage she did not pay and the nearly $500,000 kids' trust fund.

She had not yet been arrested in Washington for the attempted murder and managed to keep her job at a Virginia school even after attacking a child there in anger.

CHAPTER 19

Wendy was visiting the children's private school in Washington, D.C. when the police arrived and arrested her for attempted murder.

I had already been living in the Bahamas for some time. She hired a friend of ours from the past, a criminal lawyer, who argued to the District Attorney in Washington, D.C. that the case could not go to trial because the only witness had left the country. No one ever thought to ask me if I would come back for the trial. Wendy's lawyer's argument won the day, and she never stood trial for the attempted murder!

Kendrick ensured that Wendy would never stand trial for her thirty- odd assaults against me in Arlington, making it look as if they never happened. While I did not ask the police to press charges at the time of the assaults, immediately after the attempted murder, I asked the police through my lawyer to charge her for those attacks. Kendrick intervened to prevent that, and he managed to protect Wendy. Pretty amazing that someone who was violent and delusional and could not tell fact from fiction would get away with those attacks. It was also amazing what money could buy.

Kendrick's tyranny was over, or so I thought in April 1997. I had fired Philip, who was too scared of Kendrick to do anything other than kiss his ass. I hired Steven, a friend who had worked with me for years and sometimes did divorce cases. For me, he asked the Virginia Court of Appeals to review the verdict.

His appeal brief on my behalf was roundly excoriated by a later family lawyer, Matt, I hired, for being grossly inadequate under the extreme circumstances of the Kendrick "trial." I am afraid Steven also lacked the fortitude to take on and expose that bully in the courts.

The appeals court determined that there was a great possibility that everything Kendrick did in the case was wrong, but because he had imposed a non-participation sanction on me, I could not appeal and the decision would stand. There was no inherent logic in the appeals court's opinion. The appeals judges conceded that the trial judge was probably mistaken but refused to disturb his ruling because of an illegal non-participation sanction!

This was a judicial cop-out. The appeals judges saw a way to duck the case and jumped on it. This is the overriding problem with justice. Judges are people, and their decisions may be tainted by laziness, ignorance, bias, personal connections, conflicts or malfeasance. Artificial Intelligence might make for a better judge. When it comes to human beings, it takes a wise, dedicated, honest, experienced, well educated person to be a good judge, and those seem quite rare.

Consider how much power judges have. No one really looks over their shoulders. Sure there are appeals courts, but they do not always right all the wrongs from below. Judges, generally, may have opaque or illogical reasons for their decisions. There are few other parallel situations in society. People's lives depend on these decisions. The gravity of what these judges do is rarely matched by their integrity and excellence, and then the system can become an abomination. This was one of those times.

I never bargained to have my life and my children's determined, in fact ruined, by a judge.

Steven was supposed to appeal to the Virginia Supreme Court or at least try to, since there was no automatic right of appeal to that state's highest court. However, he missed the deadline for the Virginia Supreme Court appeal, shutting the door forever on any chance of undoing the unjust Kendrick divorce decisions. That was gross negligence on his part, and I was forever stuck with the consequences.

By way of apology, Steven told me to sue him and told his insurance company to pay me. That was as strange as anything else that had happened. The money I recovered helped a little bit, but only for a very short time. Steven's malpractice insurer was not voluntarily going to pay to fix my life.

I dealt with the divorce remotely, from the Bahamas. I had little to do directly with what was going on in the divorce and appeals courts in Virginia. I had left because I felt I had to -- because the situation was stacked against me and a malevolent judge was deciding my fate and that of my family. In all that Kendrick "tried," I was to blame, and yet I was not even involved. I stayed as far away as I could -- being closer would have been even worse.

This was in accordance with the legal advice I had been given, however unusual it might seem. Under the circumstances, it was probably correct.

CHAPTER 20

In the Bahamas, I tried everything I could think of and anything anyone else I knew could think of, to move my life forward, particularly with regard to my professional endeavors. I had accomplished so much, but there was a lot more that I could do. Also, I needed the money. I had made a lot, but I was forced to spend a great deal. Before all the troubles unfolded in the 1990s, I spent a lot to build a practice and for medical training and education as well as the costs of a family, a suburban home and private schools for the children.

I was the main provider, not Wendy, even when she was working. She certainly never contributed a penny from her secret trust funds. My parents had left me relatively little -- my mother had been a teacher and my father had worked only part time. This was 1997 and my father was still alive, although in a vegetative state.

I scoured the world for work. In Medicine, it was damn hard. You can not just pick up   and practice somewhere else -- you have to get licensed in that country. I was licensed in the United States, but I was not there anymore.

Very few countries are willing to accept American doctors, for political reasons. Other countries have their own doctors, and they do not want the competition. Also, if the United States does not a accept a medical license from another country, that country will usually not accept one from the United States.   I had worked in England during part of my training, but the medical association there now refused to let me practice, claiming, somewhat absurdly, that U.S. training was not equivalent to the training in England. The English medical license I had had at Moorfield's Eye Hospital in London had been temporary. I also did some training in Australia, but the story there was the same.

I tried a lot of countries, but the only language I could manage in was English. Other countries demanded that I take medical school exams again in their language. I was 50 years old. It had been decades since I had taken medical school exams, and much of those exams are about general medicine, and not related to the specific field in which I was working. Long experience working in a specialty meant nothing to those holding the keys to practicing in countries whose systems were rigged to protect their own.

I had created and managed successful medical companies. I was well versed in many aspects of health care delivery and in medical products. But my experience was entrepreneurial, great if I was in charge, and useless if someone else was. These companies hire MBAs right out of graduate school, not people like me. Headhunters tried to find work for me, but to no avail. Not in Canada, or in Europe, or in Australasia, or in Asia, not in big centers, not anywhere. They considered 50 to be old even though it did not seem old to me. I wanted so much to work in my field and expand my horizons. I felt I had an enormous amount to offer. I was willing to relocate to many places. There were just too many obstacles.

The Bahamas has casinos, and I had been to them in the past while on vacation. Once I was living there, the casinos stared me in the face all the time. I picked up a couple books on blackjack, the kind that guarantee that you can beat the house if you learn to play and count the cards. I decided I could do that. I learned to play, and I practiced. Then I set out on a one-year trial, playing in a structured and controlled way, to be able to scientifically test my playing hypothesis and to limit my losses in case my experiment failed. I went mostly to the hotel casino near my apartment. I played about five times a week, just like a regular job. I certainly had the time.

I used to be incredibly busy, and I needed forty-eight hours in each day. By 1998, I sometimes had trouble filling twenty-four.

I had friends in Nassau. I had played golf since I was a child, and I continued in the Bahamas. I played tennis. I played racquetball. I played as much bridge as I could find on that small island, not that there was so much. I traveled when I had the opportunity or the business or professional need, making sure not to do it extravagantly. I could not travel to the United States, which was so close, but I could go to many other places.

I decided that if I could become a damn good blackjack player, I would have a new career.

I did not do badly. Over a year of disciplined playing, I did not lose that much, but I could not consistently beat the house. I reluctantly gave up on becoming a professional blackjack player.

One evening while I was still playing at the casino, which was frequented mostly by tourists, I found myself sitting next to people who were conversing about the Buffalo, New York area town of Tonawanda, and it became clear that they were visiting from there. Wendy had grown up in Tonawanda. I had been in the Buffalo area only once in my life, with her, even though I grew up in New York City. But those two cities are five hundred miles, or eight hundred kilometers, apart.

I asked the tourists whether they had ever heard of the Richter family from the Tonawanda area. I could not believe the response. A woman, probably a few years younger than I but old enough to remember them, told me: "You don't want to get mixed up with that Richter lot." I asked what she meant, but she did not want to elaborate, saying that the story was too ugly to relate.

CHAPTER 21

By late 1998, I had gotten somewhat used to living in the Bahamas, although I knew it was not where I wanted to spend the rest of my life. In a way, it was too much of a good thing.

White sand beaches everywhere, a good climate and a slow, comfortable enough way of life. I was practicing some Medicine, still keeping involved, treating patients. The leisure activities were good. It was, after all, a vacation paradise.

Although our licensing activities for new manufacturers infringing Interlase's patents had mostly dried up, a regular, even slightly increasing stream of income was coming from the five-year-old Spectranetics license agreement. Spectranetics was perennially cheating, but by auditing its sales, making demands and threatening a lawsuit, we usually got it to fork over most of the difference between what it had voluntarily paid of the royalties and what it should have paid.

In the intellectual property/innovation business, none of the customers were voluntary. The nature of their products forced them to have to license if their products infringed the patents. These companies' willingness to pay royalties was, at best, lukewarm. But, legally, they had no choice-- so long as you could enforce your patents successfully against them. It was a constant battle, but that was just a part of the multifarious business of innovation and intellectual property.

I was responsible for keeping on top of the industry, the players, the competition, the clients' insurance or government payers, the regulators, the patent offices, new research and development in the sector and pretty much anything that affected our technology.

Since 1988, I had spent a good deal of time on this global endeavor for our partnership, whose name Art and I had changed to Interlase. While I could not find work doing these things for someone else's company, at least I was still doing it for ours.

I managed to live off our royalties, after our expenses. Our patents would not expire for another nine years, and by then I would be 60. This second career I had stumbled into in the late 1970s was paying off, at least after the dramatic patent lawsuits which had begun ten years earlier. Art and I remained close although I could never get him to visit the Bahamas. We continued to talk almost daily. He was generally quite pleased with how things were going with Interlase, although he, too, missed our hands-on experimentation and the prospect of another eureka moment.

Art had one complaint, though. After the divorce, my ex-wife had her attorneys depose him, or interview him under oath, several times over a year and a half in what is called post-judgment discovery.

My ex- wife had received a huge and unjustifiable judgment of several million dollars from the divorce. Then, there was the absurd amount of child support. She wanted to collect more on all of it, in any way she could, even beyond everything else she had gotten from me.

Shortly after the divorce was final, she walked into a Florida bank where one my companies had an account, convinced the tellers that she was my wife and, although she was not a signatory on the account, they gave her the $100,000 balance in cash. I still do not understand why she was able to withdraw it. The bank clammed up and would never speak to me afterwards. The Comptroller of the Currency, the U.S. federal bank regulator, was too busy to deal with this matter when I complained. In view of Kendrick's judgments, I was hardly in a position to sue my ex-wife for stealing that money. The bank did not suffer, although it should have for allowing Wendy's pilferage.

Wendy's lawyers unmercifully hounded Art. Where is the company money? Why can't he just get my half and hand it over to her?

Art told me that her lawyers threatened him and his family. I never knew all of the details of the depositions. Since we were excluded from the farce they called a divorce case, I never knew that Art had been deposed unless he complained about it to me.

Finally, he said, "Ken, do something about your ex- wife, she's killing me."

Funny, I thought she was killing me. Actually, it turned out, she was killing both of us!

CHAPTER 22

I still missed my children and old friends and much else that I had lost. My existence had become relatively lonely, but I was managing. For the first time in quite some time, I began to feel that I had gotten through the dark, murky period after the attack.

One day in early September 1998, Art called. That was hardly unusual. We talked about the company and other things and people. When the conversation was about to end, Art said abruptly, "Ken, I am going to miss our conversations and our friendship."

That sounded so strange, out of the blue, that I did not even respond. I just said something inappropriate like "Okay, Art, see you" and then we hung up. I began to reflect only after I put down the phone. What did Art mean? It made no sense.

I may have tried to call Art in the normal course of things during the rest of that month, but I could not get him on the phone. I went away for a couple of weeks and that probably forestalled any elucidation of this.

We usually received quarterly reports from Spectranetics, as we did for most licensee manufacturers. The end of September 1998 came and went, and there was no report. I called my contacts at the company, but I could not get through to them. I sensed they were avoiding me.

I mentioned this to Interlase's management team, a financial company we had brought in about a year and a half earlier that was based in Providenciales, in the Turks & Caicos Islands of the British West Indies, close to Nassau. This company, Lucre Investments, was run by a finance guy from Canada. We had brought him in in early 1997 when Interlase was having trouble with Spectranetics, again.

Now, we needed an investor in order to continue our research and license a few new players who were infringing our patents. It also looked like we might need to sue Spectranetics again for breaching the patent license, and that all required money.

We were looking for an equity deal for Interlase, to improve its financial position. We found it in early 1998 with White Star Holdings, the Caribbean investment arm of a British-owned company.

At Lucre's direction, I negotiated the deal for Interlase in London with the owners of White Star's parent, an English technology company. They got a percentage of Interlase in exchange for a cash infusion and their guarantees to fund any necessary patent-related litigation for the Interlase enterprise. Since I was the manager of Interlase and the world expert on its technology for intraluminal usage, the new owners asked me to continue running the operations for White Star. I still got a percentage of what Interlase received, and for me, it was not much different from before.

Lucre had people in the British West Indies, but it also had directors in Nassau, including me. Lucre made me a director from the outset since I was still running the operations on a day to day basis.

In October 1998, Lucre's lawyers, in conjunction with those for White Star, looked into Spectranetics' non-reporting for the third quarter of that year. What they found was shocking.

Spectranetics was no longer paying Interlase or White Star anything. The medical-device company claimed that litigation in Virginia prevented any payment. Spectranetics, of course, never wanted to pay to use our technology, which was in every item it ever manufactured and sold. When Spectranetics paid, it paid as little as possible, until it was forced to pay up according to the license agreement with Interlase, and now with White Star/Interlase. That is often how this industry works.

Spectranetics had been founded in the 1980s by a man who served as its chief executive officer until he was killed in a mountain-climbing accident in Colorado. During his time at the helm of Spectranetics, the company signed its original license agreement with Interlase's predecessor, Pillco, in 1993. The license remained unchanged in 1998.

The founder's successors were very different. They were, from the outset, difficult to work with and dishonorable in their intentions. They acted as if the large recurring expenditure for royalties was money they were throwing away.

They seemed to think that the royalties paid to us should have been used to pay shareholders, to re- invest in ongoing FDA and other clinical trials for new uses of their laser/catheter technology around the world, or to line their pockets for the next 15 years with lucrative stock options and stock bonuses.

It was customary for officers and directors in these companies to issue stock options and/or stock bonuses to themselves, often, and for significant sums. They might be restricted for some time from cashing in the options or bonuses, eventually, the holders got to sell.

Spectranetics has never showed a profit in its thirty years as a public company. One can only wonder about the propriety of such bonuses in those situations. Shareholders filed at least two large class action lawsuits against Spectranetics and its top management for a whole array of alleged financial defalcations. Both cases wound up with large cash settlements for the shareholders.

Spectranetics' management tried to boost the stock price by hyping reports of new clinical trials and possible new sales. That strategy is industry- wide. Then they cashed in on the multi-million-dollar insider stock deals they had previously negotiated for themselves.

Start-ups are not as well monitored by industry analysts as are larger companies. They are not as transparent to shareholders or as well diversified as bigger businesses. Most of Spectranetics' shareholders were institutional, and the ultimate beneficial owners were 401-K or other pension plan holders with little knowledge of the plans' underlying investment holdings.

The corporate insiders, starting from the top down, were too often crooked, robbing the companies and their owners, fooling analysts and regulators and even stock exchanges like the NASDAQ, for as long as they could -- until someone stopped them, they got a better job or retired on their sometimes ill-gotten gains. This is not uncommon in the start-up world.

Many of these companies do well, although most do not. Some of them are probably done in by corporate greed as much as by poor technology and products, poor management generally, markets turning against them, fierce competition, difficult or adverse regulators, clinical failures and a lack of investment capital.

Some start-ups falter because the insiders are crooks. The next to the last Spectranetics CEO went to prison, convicted of stockholder fraud and other financial crimes. The company paid for that.

In the end, Spectranetics was purchased by Royal Philips, a huge maker of medical devices and other products.

These kinds of start- up medical device companies never

pay anyone unless they have to, except for their own executives. Spectranetics nearly went under many times. It lost lawsuit after lawsuit, and many of those lawsuits were for failing to pay.

What Spectranetics paid Interlase in royalties and what it later owed us was significant for a company its size but not for a huge enterprise like Philips. In the end, Spectranetics still owed Interlase more than five million dollars.

Our immediate problem, at Interlase, at White Star and at Lucre in late 1998 was: Why had Spectranetics stopped paying? Lucre's lawyers soon found out. They hired lawyers in Virginia who discovered what had happened, and it was almost beyond belief.

CHAPTER 23

They had broken Art Coster. It was cold and calculated. Kendrick was angry about failing to put me in jail. Wendy, at least through her team of attorneys, was also unyieldingly in her demands that I be jailed.

Since April 1997, when Kendrick signed the divorce decree that he never even read, Wendy's passion for punishing me and righting all the wrongs she imagined, grew ever stronger. After April 1997, her lawyers took Art's deposition three times in a little over a year. They harangued and threatened him, alleging he was conspiring with me to prevent her from getting money that she wrongly thought should be hers.

My lawyers had had no idea these depositions were occurring and no chance to object or to participate in them. This was a corollary of the non- participation sanction that endured and ensured that the usual elements of fairness in a lawsuit were missing.

For instance, we could never record in the court how much money Wendy received to satisfy the divorce award or any award Kendrick had given in her favor. At some point, those should have been marked paid and the divorce case ended. But because I could not participate, I could not register a payment of any kind with the court. Where is the justice in that? Wendy would continue to get whatever she could, forever. I would never get credit even for the first dollar paid, much less the last. Since I could neither appeal nor participate, nothing was recorded in court for monies Wendy received and there was no way to reduce or remove the divorce award. The albatross was to remain forever around my neck. I remained forever in jeopardy and blocked from seeing my children. I continued to be held in contempt. Kendrick loved this kind of quasi-judicial terrorism.

Kendrick's bag of tricks contained more than holding me and my attorneys in contempt. Wendy's lawyers, in keeping with Kendrick's illegal judicial modus operandi, threatened Art since they could get to him. They made it very clear that he would be held in contempt if he did not make certain that the half of Interlase's revenues that would have gone to me were turned over to Wendy. Never mind that some of those revenues should have covered Interlase's expenses. Never mind that I was not supposed to get half because part of that money was supposed to go to White Star as per the deal made in early 1997. In other words, never mind any reality or any legality, just do whatever is necessary to get the money to Wendy-- and, first and foremost, to keep any of it from me.

Legally, Art could not turn over half of Interlase's revenues. His family limited partnership was only a limited partner in Interlase and did not have the power, under the partnership laws, to take that action. But he was afraid of being held in contempt by Kendrick and rotting in a jail cell in Arlington, Virginia.

I did not know in September 1998 that Art was terminally ill. He never said a word to me about it.

The cancer had spread to his brain, and questioning under oath by Wendy and her mob was the last thing he needed in his dying days. He did not want to die in Kendrick's jail. To this day, I do not know whether Wendy or her attorneys knew how ill Art was. If they had known, it probably would have made no difference to them.

Only later did I learn that Art and his lawyers were told in no uncertain terms that they had to sign over Interlase to Kendrick's court.

Wendy's lawyers, in cahoots with Kendrick, concocted a document in which Art's Coster Family Limited Partnership asked the rogue judge to appoint a receiver over Interlase. Even though the lawyer for the Coster Family Limited Partnership signed the document on that partnership's (and Art's) behalf, it was illegal because limited partners do not have the power to make such requests. Wendy's lawyers and Kendrick also made up a story claiming that "Dr. Fox spirited Interlase's monies out of the United States."

Interlase, the successor to Pillco, never had operated in the United States and had never received money in the United States, not from any licensee. Its accounts were always in the British West Indies. Since April 1997, the accounts of Interlase's new general partner, Lucre, were also in the British West Indies. Neither Interlase nor Lucre ever had accounts in the United States.

I had operated Interlase, its predecessor Pillco and also lately White Star for altogether a decade by 1998. I had lived in the Bahamas for nearly three years by the time a dying Art was coerced into agreeing to the signing of that illegal document asking Kendrick to appoint a receiver over Interlase, negating White Star's involvement.

Spectranetics was then essentially Interlase's only paying licensee. It had already been paying quarterly royalties for years to the Lucre account in the British West Indies for Interlase. Spectranetics never paid the royalties to an account for Interlase in the United States. There was nothing in the United States for Interlase -- just an out-of-control judge abetted by an out-of-control ex-wife.

So Art signed the papers, and they were submitted to Kendrick. There was no reason for Kendrick or any judge in Arlington, Virginia, or any other court in the United States to get this Interlase "case."

At the time, much of what Spectranetics was supposed to pay in royalties was supposed to go to White Star, which had no U.S. connection. Interlase was never a Virginia entity. No Virginia court could have legally had jurisdiction over it. But in Kendrick's law book, that hardly mattered.

Kendrick immediately set out to appoint a receiver for Interlase. The idea was to take control of Interlase's revenues, damn its business obligations, and divide them up by first handsomely paying the receiver and his attorneys, then giving Wendy most of the rest, making believe it was my money she was taking to satisfy her so- called divorce order. The Coster family partnership got what was left. What was left was much less than the Costers would have received otherwise and what they had been getting up until the receivership. In the end, they probably got no more than a quarter of what they deserved or would have gotten had Interlase and White Star been allowed to operate normally, and not been run into the ground by the Kendrick-appointed receiver.

That was not all that Kendrick did illegally. He held a private meeting in his chambers in the Arlington courthouse, inviting only lawyers for Wendy, the Coster group and the receiver they had selected-- a local lawyer named Richard Mendelson.

Mendelson was chosen for this mission by John Toothman, a former law associate of Art's attorney, after consultation with lawyers for my ex- wife. They used a law governing temporary receiverships for Virginia businesses, which was not meant for foreign entities. The temporary receivership was limited to 30 days under the law. This one lasted for eleven years.

A public hearing is required prior to any receivership being put in place. All parties in interest of the target entity are to be legally served and invited to the public hearing. That would, certainly, have included Lucre and myself, both partners, and it would, of course, have included notice to the (Interlase) limited partnership itself. There was no public hearing for this receivership. There was no service and no notice, either. Kendrick just signed off on it, and the receivership took full control of Interlase.

He determined then that Interlase was an "alter ego" of mine, along with dozens of other things, most of which I had never heard of and which Kendrick, or Wendy's attorneys invented for the occasion. It looked better that way, they thought.

Art was hardly in a position to say otherwise in view of the guns held to his head -- one from the outside, by my ex-wife and her henchmen, and the other, from the cancer inside. He died three months later.

When Lucre's attorneys found out about the receivership, the general partner hired a local lawyer to oppose it, reverse it and/or appeal it. Kendrick held that lawyer in contempt, forced him to disgorge his fees and ordered him jailed when he appealed the contempt citation to the Court of Appeals of Virginia.

White Star also cared. They had paid for much of Interlase and were totally ignored by this quasi- judicial chicanery. They hired counsel too. No sooner did that happen was that lawyer also held in contempt by Kendrick and his fees disgorged. They hired another local attorney, started another lawsuit and quickly the same fate befell the next guy too. Eventually, totally frustrated and disgusted with Kendrick and his form of justice in northern Virginia, White Star's British owners also gave up. White Star, a foreign company, had been summarily been put out of business by Kendrick, their investment lost, or maybe, more aptly, confiscated by this rogue court.

Mendelson, Toothman and Kendrick, with my ex- wife fully concurring, ignored the most fundamental due process required in any lawsuit: they never got jurisdiction, and they failed to serve legal notice on all interested parties. Those things are fundamental principles of natural justice anywhere in the civilized world.

Kendrick and his cronies knew they could get away with this in their parallel justice system. They knew that if we were allowed to be included and to participate, we had a very good chance of getting this whole thing overturned. So, I was never served, even though I was a limited partner of Interlase. The owners of White Star, the legitimate, commercial buyer, were never served. Lucre, Interlase's general partner, was never served. Kendrick and his gang knew where we were. Lucre and White Star were duly registered corporations with registered agents, as is normal around the world. Amazingly, Interlase LP, the direct victim of this receivership, was never served, either. It, too, had a publicly known, registered agent, in the U.S. state of Georgia.

This was not just kangaroo justice, it was as if an army of kangaroos had taken over some court in Virginia.

The contempt citations against Interlase and White Star attorneys, requested by Toothman for Mendelson, were lifted on appeal by the Virginia Court of Appeal. Those lawyers' clients -- Interlase; White Star Holdings, the patents' majority owner; Lucre Investments, the general partner of Interlase; and I had all been deprived of legal representation and any opportunity to appear in court or participate. All were owners or legal successors of Interlase, but they were simply cast aside. All were deprived of income from the enterprise.

Mendelson, and his lawyer, Toothman, did not want interlopers in the phony receivership. If there had been any higher court review, the receivership would have fallen in half a heartbeat. Lawyers sitting in Kendrick's courtroom waiting for their own cases to be heard witnessed what several of them described as the most amazing show of concerted injustice they had ever seen.

Attempts to appeal Kendrick's unnatural justice to the Virginia Supreme Court were not allowed as long as the receivership continued. The choice to hear an appeal during a receivership is a matter of the state high court's discretion and not a right. There were pitifully few legal ways to try to stop this onslaught, a key fact that Kendrick and his minions relied upon.

CHAPTER 24

Of course, Spectranetics had to play along. It had to send the quarterly payments to the court's appointed receiver, Mendelson. Spectranetics' managers soon realized that they had inadvertently fallen into a far better situation than their cheating could have brought them when I was in charge. How much Mendelson expected to receive for patent royalties or even cared about receiving was a fraction of what it should have been, and Spectranetics was the beneficiary.

A licensee company tends to have an adversarial relationship with a business to which it pays royalties and its receiver. But Spectranetics was only too happy with the receiver. By the time the patents expired, Spectranetics had saved about $10 million in royalties by underpaying Interlase under Mendelson.

Mendelson did not care. He and Toothman received volumes of writings on my behalf and that of the real Interlase and knew damn well what they should have done for Interlase, their nominal client. So, they had a pretty good idea of how much royalty income they were forsaking year after year because my lawyers and Lucre's made sure they were informed.

Why didn't Mendelson care? His real client was

Wendy, and she was spoon- fed a big chunk of what he collected over the eleven long years of his receivership. She did not need the money. She was legally entitled to none of it. She wanted to make sure that I did not get any of it; that was the point of the receivership. Mendelson collected plenty for himself, Toothman and the rest of his entourage, who all fed at this same illegal trough. They got enough to hold half a dozen attorneys in contempt if they challenged the receivership. They tied up White Star's investment and put that company out of business. They destroyed Interlase. This was Wendy's goal. The Coster family got something, but not as much as they should have. I can only hope that Art died in peace.

Kendrick issued a permanent injunction against Lucre Investments, the only general partner of Interlase LP at that time, to prevent it from ever acting again for Interlase. Lucre was not in that illegal receivership case Kendrick had invented, so Kendrick had no jurisdiction over it and was not legally entitled to make rulings concerning it. He also had no jurisdiction over Interlase LP itself and could not legally issue decisions concerning it!

The general partner of a limited partnership is like the president of a corporation. The general partner is chosen by the limited partners of a limited partnership, just as a corporation's board of directors and, ultimately, the shareholders or equity owners select their president and executive officers. But Kendrick barred Lucre, anyway. This was state confiscation of a business but without jurisdiction or due process.

Wendy collected more than a million dollars from Mendelson's tyranny, which lasted longer than any receivership in the Guinness Book of Records, even though its legal excuse for existing was a temporary receivership law in Virginia limited to one month.

The money Wendy got was deemed to be what I would have received, given Mendelson's meager collections for Interlase. Wendy decided she would attribute the money to "child support" paid on my behalf. By the end of the receivership, the youngest child was 23, far beyond the legal age for which child support is owing. If my lawyer or I had had legal and legitimate access to the court, we would have terminated the grotesquely illegal amount of child support long before then. But we did not and therefore could not. So, Wendy assumed it just continued; she imagined she would get a tremendous additional tax benefit that way.

She reported none of the money she received from Mendelson to the tax authorities, since, she conveniently reasoned, child support is not taxable income. In reality, the money was royalty income from manufacturers who required my patented technology for their products.

The Internal Revenue Service eventually investigated my ex-wife for criminal tax evasion. I found out because she demanded Mendelson use more of my money to hire another attorney to devise an excuse as to why she need not have considered the payments royalty distributions.

This sixty-thousand-dollar tax attorney opinion, a twenty-odd page work of fiction, was intended to give Wendy some cover. She had gone from attempted murder, to stealing from bank accounts, to tax evasion.

One small genetic mutation did this to someone who, a decade or two earlier, was an amazing person.

In the end she made a deal with the IRS and stayed out of jail. Her attorney bills, not to mention penalties and interest, were probably very high.

CHAPTER 25

As tumultuous as late 1998 was, 1999 turned out to be even worse.

Art died in early 1999. He had once been like a brother to me and had been my long-term partner in inventing and in business.

I had no income from Interlase. Wendy was on her way to accumulating over a million dollars of what should have been my royalties from Interlase, and I got no credit whatsoever for that toward satisfying the divorce judgment. Since the day I left our house after the attempted murder, I never saw Wendy again and I never communicated with her.

Her phony receiver and his henchmen were ripping off even more from Interlase. They were actively preventing it from earning many times what they were collecting from already extant patent licensee companies. They failed to properly extend the patents. Sometimes they did not even renew them in a timely fashion. They did not license other infringing manufacturers. Usually, they were just not bothering to do anything.

Mendelson and Toothman, who apparently had no other law clients besides Mendelson/Interlase, were stuffing it away as fast as Spectranetics would pay it-- not that fast, but fast enough that they, too, made well beyond a million dollars over the years.

Mendelson made sure that Interlase's research efforts ceased. If we had been allowed to continue, we might have made significant advances in other areas besides arteriosclerotic vascular disease and kidney stone removal. Our technology could have been employed for other medical purposes, but we needed to do the experiments. Suppose Kendrick had shut down Boston Scientific, Medtronic or some other medical powerhouse with a fake lawsuit and a fake receiver?

Lucre and I tried every way our advisers could imagine to upset this cancerous receivership that was depriving us of the use of our patents and my livelihood. Lucre, Interlase's general partner, filed for a non- debt bankruptcy in Georgia where Interlase LP had always been chartered. Being chartered, or legally domiciled, in Georgia does not mean that Interlase operated anywhere in the United States or had any business connection there.

We hoped that would trump Mendelson and replace him with a court- appointed bankruptcy trustee who might, finally, set things straight. Then, the research could continue and probably we could license our newer infringers. Also, a legitimate bankruptcy trustee could have continued to put Spectranetics' feet to the fire and force it to pay the proper royalties under the license. I was always available to advise anyone who cared to listen to impart to them what I knew. I learned even much more much more recently when, finally, previously concealed documents trickled out.

My lawyers and I informed Mendelson of this, but he was not interested in licensing others, in rectifying chronic underpayments by Spectranetics and smaller, pre- Mendelson, licensee manufacturers, or in anything else that would have been proper regarding Interlase's patents and its intellectual property business.

We had our lawyers advise Mendelson that he should extend the patents' terms and take other patent- related actions. The extension was possible because of FDA delays in approvals of licensed medical devices. The FDA had ordered lengthy clinical trials of new medical devices, holding up their sale and our receipt of royalties. The extension was meant to replace the time lost during those earlier clinical trials before the final approval. This is legal compensation for the truncation of the patent term due to FDA delays.

After the bankruptcy filing, we also informed Mendelson that some patent licenses could be renegotiated if the licensor, Interlase, was in bankruptcy. This a potentially valuable tool for a patent holder in bankruptcy. Of course, we also wanted to get rid of Mendelson and his illegal operation and the despotic rogue judge Kendrick.

We filed for Interlase's bankruptcy in Georgia, its legal domicile. Mendelson had the case moved to northern Virginia. There, the bankruptcy judge could not be persuaded to do the usual thing: allow a presumably independent bankruptcy trustee to run Interlase. Instead, he was talked into letting Mendelson continue the state court receivership, even though a federal bankruptcy then existed. In other words, the bankruptcy court "abstained."

This meant that while a nominal bankruptcy trustee was appointed, he would oversee the receiver, but would not initiate any actions on behalf of the Interlase bankruptcy estate. The bankruptcy court appointed the trustee, a lawyer called Jason Gold, in mid-1999, but Mendelson continued to run Interlase. Gold remained trustee in name only for nearly 12 more years. He submitted bills for himself and his attorneys every quarter. It was as if a bankruptcy had never occurred, except that now there were more mouths feeding at the Interlase trough.

In 2009, too late to make much of a difference, Lucre finally succeeded in getting the bankruptcy judge to realize that Mendelson was an abject failure as a receiver. Actually, he was an abject fraud, but that issue was never taken up.

Unfortunately, the bankruptcy court had not previously taken that much of an interest in the matter. In a bankruptcy, the trustee, and only the trustee, speaks for the estate -- for

Interlase LP. That silenced me, Lucre, White Star Holdings and the rest of the disadvantaged parties never included in either the receivership or the bankruptcy-- at least until many years after all royalties ceased, and the bankruptcy judge woke up.

Once the bankruptcy court was finally convinced that Mendelson was incompetent, it ordered the Arlington County state court, in mid-2009, to terminate the "temporary" eleven-year receivership.

Lucre's lawyer had told the bankruptcy court judge again and again that Mendelson was not collecting what he ought to, while every quarter, Mendelson, his attorneys, Gold, and his lawyers told the judge the opposite. For a long time, that was all the judge had cared to hear.

Late in 2011, Gold closed the bankruptcy after his final billing-- collecting for himself what money remained at Interlase. No royalties had been received after 2006 because the patents were allowed to expire prematurely.

As Gold saw this, it was just another successful bankruptcy case that had come to an end.

CHAPTER 26

The year 1999 was not much better in the Bahamas than in the Virginia courts.

I decided that as long as I was living in the Bahamas, I should learn to swim. I had been afraid of the water all my life. It took me about a year just to learn to put my head under water. I tried to convince myself that I could do it if I just kept trying. I felt the same way about overcoming the tragedy and the injustice that my family and I suffered, only that is taking even longer.

After I mastered submerging my head, I found a sympathetic swimming teacher in Nassau. I struggled through a few dozen lessons, in her pool and in the ocean. I never entirely overcame my fear of the water. After all the lessons, she said: "Ken, at least if you are at a pool cocktail party and someone pushes you in, you probably won't drown." I think she is right, but I am not anxious to test that hypothesis.

Foolishly, I decided that if I could survive the swimming lessons and then snorkeling in the Atlantic off Nassau, which I enjoyed, I could probably scuba dive. I could not have been more wrong.

I signed up for a day- long package of lessons aimed at tourists. In the morning, the instructors teach basic diving in a swimming pool; in the afternoon, they take you out in a boat to dive where the waves are gentle and the ocean is only fifteen feet deep.

I was near panic in the morning session, but I persevered

because I hate failure. In the afternoon, when the command came to jump off the side of the boat, I clung to the ropes mooring the vessel to a fixed structure. Finally, I let go and reached the ocean floor. I was in a complete panic. I did not know what to do. There was an instructor nearby, and he quickly diagnosed the situation and pulled me to the surface. He called to a colleague in the boat who swam out, attached me to a hook and towed me back to the boat. They hoisted me on board. The next thing I knew, I was lying on a mat on the deck near another student who had apparently suffered the same fate.

The instructors had seen this before. The other student and I tried to talk about what happened, but both of us were both in shock and embarrassed. Later, on shore, the instructors told me I had almost drowned.

That disaster occurred in February 1999. Not six weeks later, I was awakened one night by a lot of pain in my back. After my initial panic, I realized this was similar to my two prior episodes with kidney stones, or acute nephrolithiasis, in Washington, several years earlier. My laser technology had removed, or unblocked, kidney stones in probably millions of patients around the world. How coincidental, I mused. That did not make me feel any better in this very painful condition. It turned out I had kidney stones on both sides simultaneously. After a couple of days of agony, the stones passed.

That was in April. May was no better. I had been playing golf in the relatively quiet southwest corner of New Providence island about ten or twelve miles (seventeen kilometers) from the center of Nassau. I had previously belonged to the Atlantis Hotel's Ocean Club on Paradise Island, just across a small bridge from Nassau, where I learned to submerge myself in the large pool. But the membership had ended, and the club and its golf course were closed for years of renovations.

There were three other golf courses in the Nassau area then, although today there are others. One Saturday afternoon,

I was out alone at the South Ocean course. I rode up in my golf cart to the seventeenth tee, deep in the woods. It was a long par four, meaning that golfers are supposed to complete it in four strokes.

There was a slightly elevated tee box for the first stroke. When I had teed up my ball, two men darted out from the woods, pointing guns at my head. They were probably local drug addicts looking to rob golfers to pay for the next fix. There was no one else in sight, and they knew it. Instinctively, I put my hands up, and they frisked me. All they found was five Bahamas dollars, equal to five U.S. dollars. I had left my wallet in the glove box of the decade- old Suzuki I had bought from Avis in Nassau. I thought they were going to kill me when they did not find more money, and they seemed unsure what to do next.

One of them went through the golf bag on the cart, thinking the wallet must be in there. The other muttered that I must be lying about having no other money on me. They found a lot of golf balls and things, but no cash and no wallet. I think I even told them to take the golf cart, but that, of course, was ridiculous. It was all I could think to say at that moment. They backed away, still not sure what to do. I backed off toward the edge of the small hill of the tee box. They turned and ran towards the wooded area they had come from; I dropped to the ground and rolled down the hill, giving myself some small measure of cover. When I hit the bottom, I started running towards the sixteenth hole. They fired a couple of shots towards me, but fortunately missed. I do not know whether they intended to shoot me or just scare me.

I found two golfers on a golf cart on the sixteenth hole. I screamed and pointed and told them that there were two gunmen in the woods. They signaled for me to jump on the back of their cart, and we raced to the clubhouse.

The club was sympathetic. I found out later that this was

hardly the first time that a golfer had been robbed at gunpoint there. The staff gave me about a dozen golf shirts, two dozen golf balls and fetched the golf cart with my clubs from the seventeenth tee. They also gave me about $300 dollars in cash from their till and apologetically said that that was all that they had. They called a locksmith for me because the robbers had made off with my car and house keys.

They also called the Royal Bahamas Police. A cop came, made a report and promised an investigation. The police supposedly never found the robbers or any others who attacked golfers at that course that year.

The locksmith jump started the car, followed me home and picked the lock in my apartment, where I had duplicate house and car keys. That was the end of a nice afternoon's golf outing.

I decided to publicize the robbery locally and to write to travel publications to warn people that the golf course, which was unfenced and wide open, was not safe. There was a reasonably high crime rate in Nassau, but some places were more dangerous than others.

The golf course was owned by a resort, and its owners' lawyers sent me a threatening letter, claiming that I was defaming them. They reminded me that defamation was a crime in the Bahamas. After that, anonymous letters were sent to the press about this unsafe golf course. I think the course still exists, but I have not been back to see if it has a fence and better security.

October 1999 was another unpleasant month during that annus horribilis for me. Although Nassau usually wound up being sheltered from the worst hurricanes, Hugo was different. It was predicted to slam into Nassau, something that had not happened in decades, I had been told. I hoped it would veer off course and waited to see, not having any safe place to go. When the hurricane looked like it was heading straight for Nassau,

I contacted a friend who managed the then Sheraton Nassau, on Paradise Island beach next to the Atlantis Hotel. I assumed the hotel would be safer than my apartment, which was jutting out into the Atlantic Ocean in a beautiful setting that was probably unsafe during a hurricane, I thought. My friend invited me to spend the night of the expected Hugo onslaught at the hotel for a very cheap rate.

I arrived by car at the hotel, about twenty minutes from my flat, at about 7 p.m. I carefully parked the little Suzuki in the middle of an open field across the street, nowhere near trees or anything else that might be blown down and crush it. Good thing I did that.

My friend was especially hospitable that evening to the hotel's few guests -- a few tourists and a few locals who were looking for slightly better shelter than they might have at home.

My room was on the sixth floor with a large bay window.

By about 10 p.m., the wind was ferocious. Gusts reached nearly 140 miles per hour (225 kilometers per hour) during the night. The rain was heavy.

Palm trees are incredibly tenacious and not easily uprooted, but almost all the other trees around large parts of Nassau fell that night, littering roads, hitting houses and knocking out power lines.

Glass in the hotel started shattering. I was afraid to sleep on the bed because if the window broke, I would have been lacerated by the shards. I slept on the floor next to the side of the bed away from the window. That window did not break, but the huge skylight in the hotel's atrium lobby did. Many guests were sheltering there, and many of them were cut, some pretty badly. My friend called me during the night to help attend to the injured guests.

The hotel was half demolished by Hugo. It was then closed for about two years for repairs. My friend said it had needed remodeling anyway.

When I returned home the morning after the storm, I found a lot of water damage near the walls, ruining many files I had in cardboard boxes. Everything else inside the apartment was intact. The power was out, as it was almost everywhere on the island, and it was not restored for several days.

CHAPTER 27

In 1999, there was also a battle in the British Isles.

Once the flow of my income from Interlase and my patented technology was turned off, I had almost no income and my personal assets were severely dwindling.

My father and my brother were the only family I had left. My father was in a vegetative state, and Bob and I decided to make some new arrangements with the money he had beyond what was needed to pay for his continued custodial care in the nursing home, because it looked like he might not live much longer. Bob and I were his only heirs, and we knew that when he died, I would be forced to live off my half of the inheritance, at least for the foreseeable future, and that it needed to be protected.

The money was placed in several bank accounts outside the United States. It was painfully obvious by then that if that Virginia gang could bully Art and take anything they found in the United States, then we had better be one step ahead. After all, Kendrick operated under his own law. He systematically eliminated any opposition and deprived it of attorney representation. He was the quintessential judicial terrorist.

Even moving Dad's funds did not stop Wendy. She figured since she wiped out my assets and my Interlase income, a significant part of the Coster family income, and her own children's, it must be time to start on my father. Wendy also called some of my cousins, told them that I was a horrible person and begged for money. All this time, she had millions of dollars and at least two homes.

One day in Nassau, I got phone calls from three banks, one in the Isle of Jersey, one in the Isle of Guernsey and one in London. All had accounts for my father, half of which was destined for me if he died. I managed them for him but was not an owner. All three banks had been served by their local courts that day with Mareva injunctions in an obviously well coordinated attack. A Mareva injunction blocks the funds pending resolution of a claim that someone is making against the money in the account. Wendy, through counsel in all three jurisdictions, had placed these injunctions on Dad's money, claiming it was really mine. She alluded to her divorce judgment. It had already been paid off, but I was unable to register the payments with the authorities because of the in-perpetuity non-participation sanction against me. Wendy wanted my comatose father's money to satisfy her divorce award, which had been fully paid.

She was acting like an assassin who had already fired a dozen rounds into her victim but loads another clip to get in a few more shots for good measure. What she really wanted was for me to be destitute, and she was doing a pretty good job of making that happen.

The cases in Guernsey and Jersey were fairly quickly resolved in Dad's favor after a few months. Wendy's claim was seen as totally bogus in both jurisdictions. Nonetheless, attorneys there cost a lot.

In the case in England, the defendant bank did not give up quite so easily. It turned out that this financial institution in England had colluded with Wendy's English attorneys, who were working closely with her American lawyers, to tell her what Dad had in the accounts and help her get an injunction in the High Court in London against those funds.

I really had no money to fight this, but hundreds of thousands of dollars were in limbo and were about to be lost unless we somehow acted. My brother was not amused by this, either. My friend Dwight, who was a lawyer in Washington and had helped me a lot around the time of the divorce, recommended a law firm near London. I contacted the firm and told them my situation.

John, who became my solicitor, had an idea. He suggested I apply for legal aid in England even though I was neither English nor resident there, and even though I was the plaintiff, not the defendant, and this was a civil matter, not a criminal one. I was advised the government almost surely would not give me the aid, but somehow I got it.

The firm agreed to take what legal aid paid, which was almost nothing, unless we won. In that case, the financial institution would be stuck paying all of the fees, at the firm's regular rates. We met with Hugo, a well known barrister in England. In England, barristers act in court whereas the solicitors do most of the rest of the legal work. Hugo, somewhat like John, also thought we had little chance of winning. But he also agreed to take the case with only the legal aid, in deference to John and his firm because they often worked together.

We found out that Wendy's lawyers had fed the defendant institution's attorneys a load of rubbish about me. That had long been part of her team's usual modus operandi. It also became the strategy of anyone involved in any related case over the years, even when I was not a party to the lawsuit.

Lies, innuendo, distortions and worse were always tactics number one, two and three. The financial institution that her attorneys had co-opted had illegally given her confidential inside information about my father's account. Her people used the information to craft the injunction. This was a gross breach of confidentiality and privacy, criminal in nature. Somewhere, money had changed hands, and my ex-wife was one person who had plenty of that.

What started as an uphill battle for me turned around, and the financial institution came under great pressure when one insider cracked and confessed in open court. The conspiracy was exposed. At a pre-trial hearing, a judge in the High Court suggested he would refer the financial institution, and some of its officers and lawyers, to the Crown Prosecution Service, the U.K. criminal prosecutors. That could touch Wendy's attorneys, too, for criminal conspiracy and collusion. The tune at the defendant institution changed quickly at that time.

The defendant offered to settle with me for more than what I sought and more than what it had handed over to Wendy's lawyers. It also offered to pay all of the fees for my lawyers -- both the solicitor and barrister firms. Wendy's UK lawyers resigned immediately. I do not know if she ever repaid the money she had received from my father's account. It is possible that she did not, and so she would have wound up the big winner once again. For some people, crime pays. For her, it paid again and again.

Wendy had used the same old divorce judgment in England in an effort to collect for the umptiumph time on the same debt. Some of the money that the financial institution had illegally provided to Wendy had been given to her lawyers for her, and some had been turned over to the court instead. That was the part she claimed was for child support.

By the time I started fighting back, she had not yet gotten the court to release to her the money it was holding. Even after the financial institution lost its case, many additional hearings ensued about what to do with the money held at the Victorian Law Courts on the Strand in London. There were decisions, then appeals, more hearings, more judgments and more appeals. Wendy, despite the collusion revealed by this time, was still fighting to get another $200,000 or so for child support. She was afraid if she did not get that money, I might get it instead; that was always her worst nightmare and her best motivation.

My barrister continued the fight in the hope that, if she got this tranche of funds from the court, it would have to be credited as child support.

I remained in the Bahamas and never attended any of the hearings. John advised me each step of the way. In the end, a wise thirty-fourth judge who got involved in this matter saw through my ex- wife and her chicanery at the High Court. In court one day with Wendy's London and Washington counsel still in attendance, the judge offered to release $200,000 to Wendy for "child support," since we still could not show that she had already been paid several times over due to the permanent non- participation sanction. This was always her gimmick, to collect the same grossly inflated child support about ten times over.

But this judge had one caveat Wendy had not expected -- that the funds would not go directly to Wendy or to her lawyers. Instead, the money would go to the Virginia Department of Child Support Enforcement, a state government agency that would record the payment in the applicable state court for credit against the debt and then pay it to her. That meant the child support debt would be reduced by at least $200,000.

Wendy refused to take the money! Rather than see the child support debt trimmed by $200,000 from what I allegedly still owed, she walked away from the cash. When her lawyers announced her decision to the court, the thirty-fourth judge sat on the bench, scratched his head and said, "Now I have seen everything."

As astute at that thirty-fourth judge was, I suspect that if he had read a few transcripts from Kendrick, he would have gotten another crash course in "seeing everything."

CHAPTER 28

It was the end of 1999, more than four years after I had arrived for a short stay. I was still in Nassau, unable to find full-time work, with zero intellectual property business income and nominally in debt to my ex- wife for money she had received more than once. I was 52, going on 53.

My friends and I watched the fantastic millennial fireworks over the harbor that ushered in 2000, but I was restless and frustrated and fed up with living in "paradise."

Several months later, I got a phone call out of the blue from a medical recruiter in Atlanta, Georgia, whose company I had contacted years earlier. Some guy named Luke asked if I remembered him, and I pretended that I did. He said he had the deal of a lifetime for me, which I highly doubted. He said that a guy from the company in question, based in North Carolina, was in the United States at the moment and could explain it to me.

Ten minutes later, Kevin called. He was the head in-house recruiter for a new company called Palomar Medical Technologies, which was working with the outside recruiter in Georgia. Palomar was seeking a chief of Ophthalmology for a large project.

It was a sultry summer- like day. Kevin asked if I would give him a few minutes of my time for something that might change my life. Although I did not believe him for a minute, I sure needed a change of life.

Kevin told me tales of a country awash in oil money, which pledged at least $4 billion over fourteen years to build a huge military health-care system, covering nearly half the native population. It was the United Arab Emirates. A large number of people were being hired, and the top jobs were slated for Americans. They wanted me to head the Ophthalmology service.

He described salaries three times what could be had in the United States, benefits almost befitting a sheikh and other trappings of expatriate life in the Persian Gulf country. I had practiced Ophthalmology for nearly 25 years, and while that had been mainly in the United States, I had also worked for several years in other countries.

This offer was the last thing in the world I had anticipated, and the Emirates was a place I knew nothing about. I had been in more than one hundred countries, but I was not familiar with the Gulf.

I talked to a few friends and made up my mind. I donated my Suzuki to charity, packed my bags and three weeks later, I was in the Emirates. The country looks ultramodern and is full of foreigners. The locals, a minority in their own country, are mostly religious and conservative.

There was opulence everywhere -- grand edifices, expensive jewels, fast cars. The Emirati men were clad in white dishdasha robes while the women wore black abiyas. There were barely three hundred and fifty thousand Emiratis, who comprised a mere fifteen percent of a society that relied almost exclusively on foreign guest workers. There were Indians, Pakistanis, Filipinos, non- Gulf Arabs, other Asians, Europeans and North Americans, who each contributed in his or her own way, playing a carefully scripted role. This very conservative Moslem nation was a galaxy of contrasts and contradictions.

The health-care upgrade project was born out of a friendship between Retired U.S. Air Force General Buster Glossen and Sheikh Mohammed bin Zayed, Chief of Staff of the Emirati Military who then was a possible heir to the Abu Dhabi throne of his elderly father, Sheikh Zayed. The general and the chief of staff met during the First Gulf War.

Glossen, by his own admission, had no background or experience in health care, but he believed that with the right people, he could make anything work. Western-educated and forward-looking, Mohammed committed a minimum of four billion dollars over almost a decade and a half to newly formed Palomar. Run by Glossen's troops, it was fifty-one percent owned by some very wealthy locals, beholden to His Highness. They, too, had no medical knowledge or expertise.

Palomar was placed under contract to Sheikh Mohammed's Department of Medical Services (DMS), which had been operating the country's military health care system, such as it was. The DMS was a small cadre of highly placed colonels, with virtually no medical knowledge. They had, however, plenty of ego and influence. This huge political football, the Upgrade Project, may have been a defining moment in the career of Sheikh Mohammed bin Zayed, since he risked so much on its success.

In my first few days on the job at Zayed Military Hospital in the Emirati capital and seat of power, Abu Dhabi, I saw a plethora of contrasts. There was opulence beyond belief in meeting facilities, private receptions and at Western-

Emirati meetings. However, the military "referral" hospital was old and dilapidated and consisted of makeshift pre- fab buildings. It was scheduled for replacement by a new, world-class establishment. The antiquated, broken equipment for diagnosis and surgery, the lack of necessary items, the out-of-date medical supplies and general disorganization were almost beyond belief. There was no system for communications, appointments or medical records. The records were whatever any patient happened to bring. Patients, mostly Emirati soldiers, hung around the hospital clinics all day, or even all week, waiting to be seen. Soldiers' families were also eligible for medical treatment in the military system.

There were few specialists on staff who measured up to Western standards. There were no translators, necessary for the foreign doctors involved in the project. Few Emirati soldiers speak English, although the officers are generally proficient. Support staff was non-existent, overworked or poorly trained. The few Emirati locals employed within the military health-care system had almost no work ethic and very little training. Getting them to show up was a challenge.

I had taught and performed eye surgery in developing countries. The Emirati health-care system was even worse despite the nation's wealth and first-world economy. Abu Dhabi, the capital, is one of the wealthiest places on the planet. In desalinization, reforestation, construction, roads, infrastructure, oil drilling and banking, the Emiratis were immensely successful. The trappings of wealth were worthy of marvel. When it came to health care, the country was almost as poor as Togo or East Timor.

I was charged with designing, equipping, staffing, systematizing, stocking and organizing the eye-care system for a large and important segment of the Emirati population. I also planned preventive programs for Diabetic Retinopathy, a blinding blood vessel disease of the retina; glaucoma, a blinding disease of the optic nerves caused by too much pressure in the eyes; and amblyopia, or "lazy eye," a form of childhood blindness. These three common disorders together probably affected more than ten percent of the Emirati population.

But these programs never really got going. Emiratis inside the military command and some outside in the community, such as the local Red Crescent Society, were opposed to anything new or different. The notion of some Westerners starting some sort of community program was not yet developed in the Emirates. The time was just not yet right for these kind of things to happen in there.

When I first arrived at Zayed Military Hospital, I discovered that my private mobile phone number had been given not only to hospital and administrative personnel, but to practically every military officer. I began to get calls day and night from officers who wanted something for themselves or others -- often for patients I had never seen. They were used to exerting this type of control and demanding this sort of service.

One day I got the word that "the Judge was coming." This despised character was a Religious Court Judge imported from Morocco, which had close ties to the Emirates. He had been a high-level adviser to the sheikhs. The Judge was accompanied by a more sympathetic entourage; nonetheless, he demanded hours of unfettered attention for minor, repetitive eye problems and had been to no less than a dozen other Emirati and foreign Ophthalmologists over several years. I got along well enough with him that he once gave me a Moroccan fez, but he consumed a great deal of time unnecessarily. These kinds of systemic expectations and chronic usurpations negated in large measure my attempts to do my job.

The system was replete with people called Third Country National physicians (TCN's) from before the Update Project days. Some were excellent, others fair and many were neither. Palomar told us we must re-staff our Departments. But the Department of Medical Services blocked the interviews and hiring, citing various regulations, some of which they may have invented. The colonels from the department wanted to retain their current employees, who were selected because they were loyal and subservient. Most of the professionals lived in fear that they would be sent back to Pakistan, non-Gulf Arab countries or Sudan. There was also a small group of Europeans delighted to be in a tax haven and living a luxurious expat existence; they did not want to rock the boat, medical quality and principles notwithstanding. Together, this group was a pretty compliant lot, but not one generally representative of the modern standards of Medical care that was Palomar's mandate and Sheikh Mohammed's vision for his nation.

I tried to institute an appointment system in Ophthalmology. The powers that be were against it -- "too cumbersome for officers and too restrictive," they said. They preferred the time- honored "wasta" approach: the ones with the most influence go first and most often, and the others can wait. "What's the hurry?"

I tried to get decent capital equipment for surgery and diagnosis, or at least equipment that worked. The budgets were blocked by the DMS brass, and when they were not, purchasing was done at a very leisurely pace and channeled through DMS-related distribution sources that we in the Update Project referred to as the "brothers- in- law." Millions of Palomar dollars wound up being thrown down those bottomless pits.

I wanted supplies kept in stock, so that we would always have scissors that cut, forceps that grasped and bandages that stuck. There was too much bureaucracy, too many lines of command, and judgment and sourcing were highly questionable.

The Medical Board was a unit that determined what benefits soldiers and their families received from the Military. It was staffed by a couple of senior Palomar medical staff but a slightly larger number of DMS colonels and their compatriots. They used Palomar money to send abroad every Emirati who wanted to go away "for treatment." We had guys with hangnails who took a dozen friends and relatives, including four wives, to a German mountain retreat for a whole summer, paid for by the contract funds. This is the way it had been done for decades, and the officers and their friends were unwilling to forfeit their perks. This is not the way to run a health-care system.

The Emirates has a monarchic system that some of us referred to as "Sheikhism." In some of their looser moments, local Emirati friends agreed with this moniker. The ruling class, the major or royal sheikhs, are the government. The United Arab Emirates is the world's largest welfare state, and can afford to be. There are few Emiratis, and there is a lot of oil in Abu Dhabi. Business is controlled by the locals; by law, they must own at least fifty-one percent of everything. All businesses are controlled directly or indirectly by the ruling sheikhs. On the one hand, they don't want too much liberalism or Westernization for fear of a sea- change in political thinking that will destabilize their rule; on the other hand, they need to keep their people happy.

The Emirates has a council, or "Majlis," run by sheikhs that keeps most Emiratis happy. Before oil, even before the Emirates became a country, and before it had roads, schools, a written language and a recorded history, all of this less than sixty years before my time in the Emirates, Bedouins there had the camel they rode and not much else. Today, Abu Dhabi Emirate still has Bedouins, many of whom I saw as patients because their sons are soldiers. But now they might have a farm with a thousand camels, water and greenery, eighty Pakistani workers to tend their enterprises, cell phones, and a big ranch house. When they go to the Majlis they might ask for new tires for their fleet of four by fours. Important tribal elders and their constituents can obtain almost anything they want at the Majlis. They do not know much about health care, and if they get sick, they just want to go to London or Baltimore or somewhere else abroad for a month or two.

The Emirates is an intensely Moslem country. There is no overt extremism, and the State controls religion. There are generally no mullahs or imams with radical political messages. That would be too dangerous and upset the country's carefully controlled political stability. However, if you need to hospitalize a local during Ramadan, the Moslem holy month with daytime fasting, forget it. They refuse to take medicine during the daytime in that month, even if they might die, or go blind from uncontrolled glaucoma.

My plans for a new Eye Clinic were quashed. We did not have enough money for duplicate facilities for male and female patients, who, by tradition, must be compartmentalized. The $4 billion was enough to build one great system, but how much is needed for two separate ones? Some acutely ill patients, female dependents, refused to see me because I was a male physician. These ideas are very hard to change.

We needed certain pharmaceutical items stocked in the Zayed Military Hospital Pharmacy. Almost half the Palomar staff was nearly sent packing one day when the Emirati general in charge of the Department of Medical Services, a General Khalil, got exercised that his mother, who had been my patient at one time, could not get something in the Pharmacy. The strange part is guys like Khalil could buy a million of whatever she wanted on the open market, but they do not always think that way. Tradition. Control. Parochialism. Whatever the reason.

Palomar tried hard to get the necessary pharmaceuticals at a reasonable cost. When it was forced to buy from a colonel's brother's "pharmaceutical supply business," the results were often counterproductive, and the company got ripped off.

Palomar was about the largest private employer in the Emirates, with a staff of nearly three thousand. The company held staff meetings, until they were prohibited by the Department of Medical Services, which claimed they were a waste of time that should be spent seeing patients. The real reason may have had much more to do with control.

After a while, telephone communication within the hospital, including by mobile phone, was blocked by the Military, which claimed that we wasted too much time talking to each other.

The DMS had signed a contract with Philip Holtzmann, a major German company, to maintain medical equipment at the military medical facilities. Holtzmann was given responsibility for some specialized items that it had no familiarity with, such as certain sensitive Ophthalmic equipment, and other equipment that it had not expected to have to maintain. So the equipment suffered from neglect, then from disuse. Holtzmann later declared bankruptcy in Germany, perhaps because the Emiratis failed to pay it tens of millions of dollars.

That routine of contract breaches was typical. It had significant adverse impact on many well known foreign companies that did business with the United Arab Emirates. From the Palomar period alone, several hundred lawsuits were filed in Abu Dhabi courts to recover contract funds not paid to Western professionals, businesses and institutions.

Palomar purchase orders for maintenance and other needs were many times countermanded by the Department of Medical Services. This tied up Palomar and paralyzed the health care system's operations.

The DMS assigned one of its own to "equal authority" with a Palomar person at all levels, including many clinical departments. This thwarted the progress of the Upgrade Contract and maintained undue control by the DMS, ensuring the status quo remained in place. The DMS justified this as necessary oversight.

In most instances, DMS would assign to a Palomar clinical department head, a local co-chief with parallel power who had finished only six months or a year of clinical training. The Palomar employee recruited for that position was fully trained, experienced and qualified. This shadow system was destructive financially and professionally and, in the end, helped sabotage the Update Project.

Patients sent abroad went to Upgrade Project affiliated institutions such as Johns Hopkins University Medical Center in Baltimore, Maryland, which was owed hundreds of millions of dollars for health-care services. The DMS held up or commandeered the funds.

The DMS chief, Colonel Khalil, looked somewhat like a slightly younger Yassir Arafat. He had great political acumen, knew nothing about Medicine and seemed to care even less.

For most of my time at Zayed, Colonel Abdullah was the Hospital Commander. He had no Medical training and seemed proud of that. He despised the Western physicians and seemed to spend much of his time finding ways to try to show us up or undercut us. In the end, he was retired. His underling, Colonel Rashid, was a physician of modest training. He had a pleasant demeanor, but left me with the feeling that beneath it he also resented the Western-trained physicians and administrators and felt he was out of his league. He could be quite vengeful if only given half an opportunity. For instance, vacations promised to staff were sometimes canceled at the last minute by Rashid, or at least he tried to do that. These were the chief DMS military brass, at least those at the main hospital, Zayed Military Hospital, whom we dealt with daily. In the end, the "culture clash" destroyed the Upgrade Contract.

Near the end of the Upgrade Contract's first clinical year and a year and a half after Palomar came in, there were cries of "foul" from every quarter. The local partners accused General Glossen of siphoning off millions of dollars through a bevy of independent subcontractors. Palomar accused the DMS of graft, corruption and bad faith. The local partner, with the fifty-one percent nominal interest in Palomar, was alleged to have concluded self-serving deals on housing and vehicles for staff, to the tune of millions of dollars.

The truth may never be fully sorted out.

Glossen went back to North Carolina. Palomar was disbanded. Most of us beat it out of the United Arab Emirates as soon as possible after the axe fell on the Upgrade Contract. The local partner went back to his other local multi- million-dollar businesses. And the DMS, at least in late 2001, went back to "operating" a health care system that was anything but modern.

There was a tragic and pervasive unfamiliarity with the essentials for any decent health care system, and most proposed changes threatened the status quo. Good health care systems must include patient education, illness prevention and wellbeing, as well as ensuring physician and other health professional compassion, responsiveness, innovation and excellence. What won in the end there was tradition, power, control, obeisance, parochialism, greed and suspicion of almost anything foreign or new. This was a top- down, systemic problem.

The DMS had ultimate and absolute control of all that happened in the system. The rank-and-file soldier or dependent had little experience with anything other than what the superiors doled out.

The health- care system in the United Arab Emirates was difficult, if not impossible, to improve. The Palomar project collapse showed how a small, elite group in the upper Military echelon could destroy one of their leader's great visions.

Sheikhs at the highest levels saw that the health care system needed significant improvement and committed a large amount of money to accomplishing this.

Money can buy impressive equipment. Outside contractors can construct buildings and roads and make the desert green. But money can not change people's way of thinking as easily. Sheikh Mohammed bin Zayed's dream of a world class United Arab Emirates Military health care system was not to be. At least not then. And that was unfortunate for the Emirati people.

CHAPTER 29

My position in the Emirates came to an abrupt end. Another clinical situation remotely like it was not to be found.

After I left the Emirates I taught a little, but it did not pay much. I developed a new course for MBA students: the management of innovative medical technology. I drew upon my more than fifteen years in that business. Some of my students would probably wind up in health care or health products management. The overall health industry accounts for approximately fifteen percent of the world's gross domestic product. The field has huge growth potential.

Professionally, I was stymied for the remainder of my 50s and into my early 60s. Had I been able to safely return to the United States, with its huge market, I might have been able to continue practicing Ophthalmology. I still had valid medical licenses in quite a few states.

But no lawyer could assure me that I would not be arrested. That was not only because Kendrick had made a practice of holding me in contempt whenever he felt like it but also because of the exorbitant child support payments that could never be marked paid. Nonpayment of child support remained a U.S. federal crime for which there was no defense. There is no such thing as you already paid or that you can not. I had paid over and over, but I remained locked out of the courts because of the non-participation sanction. Also, there was that equally illegal writ of ne exeat, which meant if I ever set foot in Virginia, I would have to pay $1 million to leave. That was hardly the kind of justice that would encourage anyone to return, and that, of course, was what my ex-wife wanted all along.

I don't recall ever having met Kendrick, but he prevented me from living in the United States and from making a living there. He also, quite intentionally, broke up my otherwise loving family. Practicing Medicine from inside an Arlington, Virginia jail cell or from a federal prison was not my idea of a future. I gave up on the notion of returning to the United States. I had plenty of attorneys who continued to advise me not to return under those seemingly immutable, though grotesquely unjust circumstances.

I met a fantastic woman, and we have been together now almost twenty years. We met after the Emirates adventure, more than five years since everything blew up in my face in the United States. It was time.

Mendelson and Gold and their minions continued to pretend they were managing Interlase. They were highly paid to do nothing. Spectranetics and other more minor infringing manufacturers, who were never licensed to the Fox patents, but should have been, loved every minute of the free ride they got from those two.

Our lawyers and I had already spent years trying to dislodge the pair in order to change this situation. Each year, Interlase lost about a million dollars in revenues. The corrupt Kendrick had set all of this up under the cover of a judicial authority he had so sorely abused.

Under Mendelson and Gold, Interlase's revenues dwindled as Spectranetics' management took more and more liberties with royalty payments, going from paying ninety percent of what was owed through late 1998 to as little as twenty-five percent by around 2003 and thereafter. There as no longer enough money for Mendelson, Gold and their attorneys to siphon off every quarter in compensation for their gross negligence. They had finally begun to starve themselves out.

I watched from the periphery, helpless, my hands tied by the tyranny of that grand conspiracy. I began to imagine a time when the bankruptcy judge who had been sitting on his hands for years while Mendelson and his lawyers played in the sandbox with their plastic shovels, might finally decide that the so-called receivership was useless, and terminate it. Lucre militated for that. But Interlase, through its general partner, Lucre, was almost totally ignored during most of the bankruptcy.

My personal reputation had been dragged through the mud by Kendrick and his entourage as part of their scheme, and this tainted our every effort to rescue Interlase. In addition, nothing Lucre and I tried bore fruit quickly. Lucre turned its attention to Spectranetics and the years of gross underpayments of royalties. Spectranetics owed Interlase millions of dollars.

In the heady days when I ran the enterprise, we audited Spectranetics, as we were periodically allowed to do under the patent license agreement. This is customary in royalty licensing situations, since there are often significant underpayments reported and made by manufacturer patent licensees. When necessary, we had sued them for the money.

Mendelson generally was not interested in doing that and was too inept to do so anyhow. Gold was happy to allow Mendelson to continue to do nothing.

When Lucre came on board back in 1997, it was not paid a lot to get involved. Instead, it agreed to a bonus package-- a share of increased royalty revenues that Interlase or its assignees such as White Star received. This was intended as an incentive, a fairly common type of one.

Lucre was illegally enjoined from acting for Interlase, at least in the United States, by Kendrick's 1998 order. But Lucre could sue Spectranetics for grossly interfering with its bonus package by not paying Interlase enough under the Mendelson receivership. The underpayment hurt both Interlase and Lucre.

Lucre sued Spectranetics in the Netherlands, using the

manufacturer's Dutch subsidiary to get jurisdiction there. The Dutch courts are notoriously slow, so slow that the underfunding of those courts is huge news in that country these days, a national disgrace. Sometimes years go by in the Dutch courts without anything happening. The judicial budget was cut there even more in recent years apparently. The judges, who are civil servants, say they are overwhelmed by too many cases.

The trial court there did not like foreign cases, and this lawsuit meant the Dutch judges had to apply Virginia state and U.S. federal law. After many years of back and forth, the three-judge panel either got confused by the foreign laws governing the tort case or wanted to be confused by it. The court bought some arcane point of Virginia law put forward by Spectranetics that concerned only real estate and not patents or other intellectual property at all. The judge's threw out Lucre's complaint, which, by then, was worth millions of dollars. The outcome paralleled what had happened in the Virginia courts and was enormously deflating.

In a large and later case in the Netherlands, Interlase sued Spectranetics and its Dutch subsidiary for breach of contract for underpaying royalties over so many years. The action was worth ten million dollars in prior royalty shortfalls and interest. The lawsuit became possible only after Interlase's bankruptcy ended in late 2011. Then, Lucre was back in charge of Interlase at long last, after the dozen year tenure of the totally useless bankruptcy trustee had finally ended, having tied up Interlase completely during that whole period.

The bankruptcy judge had finally gotten rid of the receivership in 2009, deciding belatedly that he was fed up with Mendelson's inaction and ineffectiveness. Two years later, in late 2011, Gold finally ended the bankruptcy when he ran out of

Interlase money with which to pay himself any longer. At that point, thirteen years after the tyranny had begun, Interlase was finally freed.

The U.S. bankruptcy system is in large measure a farce. The trustees can do nothing in many cases and often seem to know nothing about what to do when there is actually money to be made from an otherwise bankrupt enterprise.

Interlase's bankruptcy was triggered not because it owed anyone even a dollar, but because we were desperate to get rid of Mendelson, the fake receiver appointed by Kendrick at the behest of my ex-wife. Trustees and receivers are supposed to hire experts to advise them on business matters they are charged with to manage. In practice, so long as there is enough money for their own fees and for their lawyers', they often do not really care. Worse, too often, they really have no one to seriously answer to. In the case of Kendrick, that could not have been more true.

In 2011, Interlase swung back into action. We lined up experts in accounting, patent law and damages and technical experts in the medical usage of Spectranetics' products. We began to puzzle out how that company had faked lower revenues as an excuse for the greatly reduced royalties it had paid Mendelson for so many years.

Mendelson never cared or was happy to get reduced revenues-- as long as there was never enough income coming in so that I would have to get something as a partner of Interlase-- after all of the others received their cuts as he had rigged it to be-- that is after the receiver and his attorneys, Gold and his lawyers, my ex-wife and the Costers got something, even if that was very little.

How many times over could the same divorce award be paid? Once, twice, three times? Beyond that, Mendelson might have to pay me something as a limited partner of Interlase with at least about a half interest in it since the very beginning. Mendelson, Wendy and Kendrick were determined that that would never happen.

The tricks Spectranetics pulled were unbelievable, as we were later able to discover. Its managers invented phony fees and categories to make it look like they got less for selling our patented products than they actually received from their customers around the world. They invented training fees, set- up fees, extra service fees and teaching fees, and more. Interlase's lawyers and I, after quite a number of years wherein Spectranetics' documents were hidden or obscured, discovered in documents from other litigation many of the so- called reports the manufacturer- licensee had given to Mendelson which had been kept from us for much more than a decade.

Spectranetics, it turned out, had also renamed some of their catheters and stopped paying royalties on them, making believe that they were not the same, otherwise infringing products they always had been. For example, the company started calling its Vitesse catheter "PELA", an acronym for a clinical trial using it, and said (to Mendelson) that the product no longer infringed and was not covered by the license agreement. The only difference between the two catheters was the name used for commercial purposes. It still infringed, and it was still fully royalty- able, according to the license agreement, which had never changed. So Spectranetics got down to as little as about twenty- five percent of the actual royalties, with a consequent shortfall of millions of dollars. Interlase's team sued for all of it. Mendelson had long been deceived by this fraud perpetrated by Spectranetics, all of which they concealed for as long as possible.

The Dutch courts spent years doing very little with the case, then threw it out, claiming that there was no proof that Art Coster had agreed that Lucre could become Interlase's replacement general partner back in 1997. That was, at best, a technical point that did not speak to the enormous fraud Spectranetics had been engaging in for years. But, according to the rules of the partnership, its internal agreement, and to the governing applicable Georgia law, the limited partner could not veto the appointment of a general partner by the majority of limited partners. In any case, Coster had specifically agreed to Lucre's appointment, as any then limited partner should reasonably have done under those circumstances extant in 1997 for good financial and management reasons. After the case was thrown out, I found a copy of a letter from Art agreeing to Lucre as general partner of Interlase, from 1997. That letter had been sitting in a box of documents in a lawyer's office in the United States.

At the time of this writing we are appealing to a higher court in the Netherlands, awaiting, we hope, a trial on the merits of Spectranetics' gross shortfalls in royalty payments. If that is accorded, we believe almost surely we will win since there remains no defense available.

More than fifteen years have past since the first lawsuit was brought against Spectranetics in the Dutch courts. Spectranetics has engineered delays time and again, whether it was because one of its lawyers was planning a wedding or because none of its attorneys, a large firm indeed that it is, were 'available' to go to court for months on end. So far it has not yet had to explain why it paid Interlase so little for so long. Hopefully, very soon, that day will finally arrive-- and Spectranetics, akin to the Emperor's new clothes, will have no answer for their many years of gross foibles. In the meanwhile Interlase's interests in the case have been taken over by investors who can better afford to carry on this litigation. Amid all of these delays, Spectranetics was purchased by Royal Philips.

CHAPTER 30

The bankruptcy lasted twelve and a half years, extremely long for any bankruptcy, but especially lengthy because Interlase did not have any debts. When the bankruptcy was finally wound up late in 2011, the general partner, in consultation with me, considered how it could finally take action against Mendelson and related defendants for failing to collect tens of millions of dollars in revenues over as much as thirteen years. In the United States, as long as a bankruptcy is ongoing, only the bankruptcy trustee can act for the debtor, including in court, even if it owes no money. While most bankruptcies concern indebted individuals or businesses, a smaller number are for other reasons, as was the case with Interlase.

The bankruptcy system is set up so that a trustee may do very little and charge the debtor for the effort. After the trustee and his lawyers are paid, what is left goes to those to whom the debtor owes money. The actual debtor, or bankrupt party, has little or no say in what the trustee does, or does not do.

In 2016 Interlase finally located a lawyer who sues way-ward attorneys on a contingency fee. It sued Mendelson and certain related parties involved in the multi-year disastrous re-ceivership in U.S. federal court for gross negligence during their long and costly tyranny over Interlase. Mendelson had died by the time of the court filing, necessitating claims against his es-tate, his trust and against his former law firm, all of which had been padded during his lifetime with Interlase's money. It took a long time after the bankruptcy had finally ended to unravel what had happened, and, crucially, all that had never happened, but should have! During the many long years of their control, neither Mendelson, nor Gold, nor anyone ever provided us with a single sentence to explain what they had done (and not done) over all of that time. Of course we had asked on many occasions and in many ways. Naturally, it was never their intention to communicate any of that to anyone, and certainly most of all, not to me.

In suing Mendelson, once again, Interlase, as I had been before, was totally outnumbered. Insurers and others on the defense side paid for many attorneys to pool their efforts to try to blunt any legal assault against their defendant clients and to overwhelm us with our meager resources. In addition to the built-in court delays, the defendants always sought as many de-lays as they could to avoid having to explain the inexplicable. These cases are always nearly interminable, that, too, meant to overwhelm the plaintiff-side seeking legal retribution for enormous damages it suffered. The costs to pursue justice are staggering.

If Spectranetics, its predecessor LAIS, USCI and other in-fringing manufacturers who lied about their royalties, their corporate, sometimes infringing, activities and even their intentions, and Mendelson and others, who did everything wrong, or their insurers, decided to pay Interlase for what had happened to it at their collective hands, it would have cost them a lot less money than having to pay all of their lawyers and others, and ours. But, they often don't look at it like that, just assuming they will prevail and their opponents will be vanquished. Or simply that justice will just never be done. Sometimes, I don't think they even think about it at all, they just obfuscate and dissemble, over and over again.

The main thrust of any would- be defense on behalf of Mendelson and even the others was always centered around the array of illegal 1998 Kendrick orders barring Lucre from authorizing a lawsuit on behalf of Interlase. Those orders were issued to prevent anyone from interfering with Kendrickian justice, such as it always was. But Kendrick did not ever have jurisdiction over Lucre and so could not legally order it to refrain from acting as Interlase's general partner, which it was since early 1997. But in the end, overcoming Kendrick's illegal orders of 1998 would require some judge to take the larger and longer view of what Kendrick had done, so as to not be blinded by all of that gross injustice. Either the judges would have to ignore all of that since none of it was legal, all of it done *ultra vires*, or totally without jurisdiction of his court, or they would have to strike it down as such. Kendrick, himself, was generally protected by 'judicial immunity' for his actions as a sitting judge, even if his motives were as totally improper as his means, and his actions based in his total corruption.

Any judge could well realize that if Mendelson's receivership, for instance, were to actually go on trial, and Interlase has asked for a jury, since there is no defense for what was actually done (and not done) under the law, Kendrick's justice, itself, even in part the Virginia legal system which put him in place and maintained him there for so long, would also be on trial. The implications of a case against Mendelson, as gross as his actions were, is clearly much larger than the tens of millions of dollars in damages he had caused. Even 20 years on, the defense was desperately hawking the previous illegal justice of Kendrick to thwart Interlase and its minions even now. They have no real defense, and if Interlase ever did receive its proverbial 'day in court', the defendants would go down in flames, in grand fashion.

Although the assault rendered by Kendrick against Lucre, against myself first and foremost, and against others to thwart Interlase and other legitimate claimants who were systemically wronged by his accomplices over so many years has not yet been overcome, Interlase and those in league with it have others who can act for the partnership and for its interests, all of that quite normal and legal. At the time of this writing, also in the U.S. federal court in Virginia, that is what is being attempted, against the Mendelson defendants, all of that quite significant against a court- appointed receiver who did abysmal things to totally vitiate a promising and already quite successful international intellectual property company.

As in the legal battle in Britain in 1999, we are still awaiting that 'thirty- fourth judge' who ultimately got that justice done right there. Also, we can harken back even further to the justice rendered by Judge Bryan in the LAIS case, now some 27 years ago, in this same U.S. federal court in Virginia, who did the same. I have learned the hard way that those judicial gems are rare, but if you are lucky enough to find them, they surely do shine brightly.

The publishing heiress Patty Hearst, who was kidnapped by the Symbionese Liberation Army in 1974, was later imprisoned for her alleged role in an SLA robbery. Hearst said that she had been abused and brainwashed by the SLA and that she was their victim rather than a perpetrator. She was convicted, but later received a presidential pardon. After Hearst left prison, she said in a national television interview: "In the justice system there is no justice, only winners and losers." I can't say that I have heard anyone say it better.

EPILOGUE

This is a story about how my life was turned upside down by a cascade of events triggered by something smaller than a knife's point-- a genetic mutation. It is also about society's failure to properly handle the mentally ill and about an abuse of justice carried out with utter impunity. Society is made up of individuals, some of them well intentioned but who often fail to fight for what is right. For that, all of us bear some measure of blame.

The story is factual according to my understanding of events and to my best recollection over many years and to what documents were available to me to which to refer. Certain portions of the story were written, of necessity, to accommodate certain privacy requirements and exigencies of readability. Other events were excluded for lack of space.